THE
VEGAN
MIDDLE EASTERN
COOKBOOK

60 IRRESISTIBLE, PLANT-BASED RECIPES
FROM NORTH AFRICA, THE LEVANT,
THE ARABIAN PENINSULA AND BEYOND

THE
VEGAN
MIDDLE EASTERN
COOKBOOK

NOHA ELBADRY-CLOUD, CREATOR OF LEEKSNBEETS

PAGE STREET
PUBLISHING CO.

PAGE STREET
PUBLISHING CO.

First published in 2023 by
Page Street Publishing Co.
27 Congress Street, Suite 1511
Salem, MA 01970
www.pagestreetpublishing.com

Distributed by Macmillan, sales in Canada by The Canadian Manda Group.

27   26   25   24   23   1 2 3 4 5

ISBN-13: 978-1-64567-886-1
ISBN-10: 1-64567-886-5

Library of Congress Control Number: 2022948031

Cover and book design by Molly Kate Young for Page Street Publishing Co.
Photography by Noha Elbadry-Cloud

Printed and bound in the United States

Page Street Publishing protects our planet by donating to nonprofits like The Trustees, which focuses on local land conservation.

DEDICATION

To John, my husband and the best sous-chef and taste-tester I could ask for, and my mom, who showed me the beauty of Middle Eastern cooking.

TABLE OF CONTENTS

INTRODUCTION

Hi there, and welcome to my cookbook. I'm so happy to have you along with me for a vegan exploration of Middle Eastern food. Aside from the basics, such as hummus and falafel, there aren't many places where you can find traditional Middle Eastern dishes made vegan, so this book was a dive into the unknown. It turned out to be far more enjoyable and doable than I could've expected, and I'm absolutely delighted that I get to share it with you!

I first started @leeksnbeets when my husband became a vegan. It was a way to chronicle my attempts to create wholesome, delicious, plant-based meals. I didn't think vegan food could be versatile or particularly tasty, but I quickly learned I was wrong. Within six months, I adopted a plant-based diet myself. At first, I considered Middle Eastern cuisine to be intrinsically opposed to a vegan lifestyle, but I soon discovered that was also a misconception.

I'm Egyptian, but I grew up in Saudi Arabia, where I was fortunate enough to attend international schools that had students from all corners of the Middle East. My exposure to Middle Eastern ingredients was vast. This came in handy because I realized that many of the flavors of Middle Eastern cuisine came from plant-based sources. From there, I devoted much of my time in the kitchen to crafting vegan versions of Middle Eastern classics and to creating recipes of my own using Middle Eastern flavors. I'm so excited for you to try them!

I've found that almost any Middle Eastern recipe can be veganized by using the right spices and making the correct swaps. It might seem overwhelming initially, but I'm here to walk you through it and show you how simple it can be. Whether you're just beginning, new to veganism or Middle Eastern food, or an expert in one or both, I hope you'll find new recipes here to try and love!

Noha Elbadry-Cloud

MIDDLE EASTERN AND VEGAN PANTRY ESSENTIALS

In this section, you'll find the arsenal of ingredients I always have in my kitchen so that I can whip up a wide range of recipes at a moment's notice. The ingredients can be divided into two categories: Middle Eastern essentials and vegan essentials—and there's plenty of overlap. What I love about these ingredients is that most of them are shelf-stable and can last for quite a while. They're also versatile and absolutely delicious!

Spices

Spices are at the heart of Middle Eastern cuisines. From Moroccan Ras el Hanout (page 41) to Lebanese 7 Spice (page 45) to Libyan Hararat (page 50), every region has its own quintessential mix. These spice blends can elevate and add incredible depth to the simplest of ingredients.

Even though most spice mixes share many of the same ingredients, often the distinction lies in the quantity of each spice in a given mix. In the Middle East, you can purchase different spice mixes at delightfully old-fashioned apothecaries, but I've gotten into the habit of making my own here in the United States. I highly recommend you make your own, too, because it gives you control over the quality and freshness—and it is just fun.

The spices I recommend having on hand for Middle Eastern cooking are:

- Aleppo pepper
- Allspice
- Caraway
- Cardamom
- Cinnamon
- Coriander
- Cumin
- Ground ginger
- Nutmeg
- Paprika (sweet and smoked)
- Saffron
- Sumac
- Turmeric

The only spice mix I prefer to buy is za'atar because the wild thyme used in it is both expensive and difficult to find.

Pastes, Sauces, Syrups and Preserved Ingredients

These ingredients are used in a variety of dishes and cuisines, and they are ones I can't cook without. The following have unique flavors and qualities that I think can't be substituted:

- Blossom water
- Grapevine leaves
- Harissa paste
- Pomegranate molasses
- Preserved lemons
- Rose water
- Tahini (preferably runny)

While many can't be found at your local supermarket, these ingredients are all easy to find at Middle Eastern/world markets or online.

Vegan Protein

Nowadays there are so many mock meats to choose from, but I try to use them sparingly because they're often costly and highly processed. Hands down my favorite vegan "meat" is homemade seitan. I find it superior in flavor, texture and nutrition, and it is super versatile. Making it can seem intimidating, but I offer various recipes for it in this book. The Juicy "Chicken" (page 24), Succulent "Steak" (page 27) and Kebab Skewers (page 64) show just how easy it is to make.

The primary ingredient in seitan is vital wheat gluten, and I recommend you always have it on hand. Other sources of vegan protein I use extensively are:

- Legumes, especially chickpeas, broad (fava) beans and lentils
- Tempeh
- Tofu (regular and silken)
- TVP (textured vegetable protein)
- Young green jackfruit

Grains and Pasta

As with many world cuisines, rice is a foundational ingredient. Having basmati and long-grain white rice on hand is a must. Rice is used in iconic dishes such as Kabsa (page 31) and Maqluba (page 51). In addition, Middle Eastern cuisine is home to a wonderful array of wholesome grains and pasta. Many of the recipes in this book—such as Tabbouleh (page 99), Kibbeh Nayeh (page 141), Freekeh–Medjool Date Salad (page 115) and Basbousa (page 153)—highlight them.

Grains and pasta to have in your pantry include:

- Bulgur (fine and coarse)
- Couscous
- Freekeh
- Maftoul (similar to pearl couscous)
- Pearl couscous
- Semolina
- Sha'ariya (vermicelli)

Quinoa, orzo and elbow pasta also are used in many of the recipes, such as Orzo Harira (page 95) and Koshary (page 59).

Other Essentials

These are ingredients you might already have on hand, but they are worth mentioning nonetheless. The essentials include:

- Extra virgin olive oil
- Kalamata olives
- Medjool dates
- Nutritional yeast
- Raw nuts and seeds, especially pistachios, almonds, pine nuts and nigella seeds
- Sun-dried tomatoes

The quality makes a big difference, so you might want to invest in pricier brands if it feels doable to you.

ICONIC BASICS

The recipes in this section are like the perfect pair of jeans—delightful in their simplicity as is, and even better when paired or prepped with other ingredients. In fact, you'd end up with a marvelous meal if you put together a spread of The Best Pita Bread (page 19), Rice with Vermicelli (page 20) and Loaded Green Salad (page 23) with either the Juicy "Chicken" (page 24) or Succulent "Steak" (page 27).

The first three recipes of the chapter are sides that are served with most Middle Eastern meals. They're naturally vegan, and the rice and salad are easy to throw together in a pinch. The pita bread recipe is more intensive, but it's worth every second because homemade bread is simply unbeatable.

The second part of the chapter features my recipes for "chicken" seitan and "steak" seitan. Much like tofu, the seitan recipes are blank canvases: good just fried up or grilled, then lightly seasoned or marinated and prepped with different ingredients. My seitan combines vital wheat gluten—a natural protein found in wheat that has a pleasantly elastic meaty texture—with legumes and seasonings. The result is high in plant-based protein and free from the preservatives and questionable ingredients found in store-bought alternatives.

Make both seitan recipes in large batches to store in your freezer for recipes such as "Chicken" Mbakbaka (page 45) or Beef-Style Seitan Shawarma Wraps (page 60). They also are great in the Seitan, Swiss Chard and Chickpea Sumakiyah (page 91) or as protein in just about any meal.

All the recipes in this section are a hit among plant-based family members and friends—and also among omnivorous ones, kids included. I hope you enjoy them just as much!

THE BEST PITA BREAD

Every Middle Eastern country has its own version of flatbread that is foundational to its cuisine. In fact, it's common for it to be served at every meal. Pita bread is the most widespread and popular of Middle Eastern flatbreads, which is no surprise. It's fluffy and pairs well with savory and sweet ingredients; it can be toasted, fried or grilled, folded into a wrap or halved to make pockets. In short, it is as delicious as it is versatile. While you can easily purchase it from most supermarkets, nothing beats the soft, pillowy goodness and cozy vibes of homemade pita bread. While this version requires a bit of patience, it's easy, straightforward and so satisfying.

YIELD: 6 TO 10 LOAVES

2½ tsp (10 g) active dry yeast

2 tsp (10 g) granulated sugar

3 tbsp (45 ml) extra virgin olive oil, plus 1 tsp for greasing

1 tsp sea salt

⅓ cup (40 g) spelt or whole-wheat flour

2⅓ cups (292 g) all-purpose flour, plus more for dusting

In a large bowl, whisk together the yeast and sugar with 1 cup (240 ml) of warm water. Let it sit until a bubbly, foamy layer forms indicating the yeast is active, 5 to 10 minutes.

Add the oil, salt and spelt flour and mix together using a spatula. Add the all-purpose flour. Mix with a spatula just until the dough comes together. Transfer the dough to a floured surface and knead by hand for 5 to 10 minutes, or until moist and elastic but no longer sticky. Place the dough in a clean bowl greased with the remaining 1 teaspoon of oil. Cover the dough with a damp kitchen towel and place it in a warm, dark spot to rise.

Once the dough has doubled in size, about 1 hour later, punch it down, transfer it to a floured surface and divide it equally into six large, eight medium or ten small portions. I weigh my dough portions, but eyeballing them is perfectly fine. Roll each portion into a ball, cover them with a damp kitchen towel and let them rest for 20 minutes.

Place a large sheet pan in the oven and preheat it to 525°F (275°C).

Taking one dough ball at a time, use a rolling pin to flatten it into a disk no thicker than ¼ inch (6 mm) and anywhere between 6 to 8 inches (15 to 20 cm) wide. Cover the disks with a damp kitchen towel and let them rest for 15 minutes.

Bake the pitas in batches on the heated sheet pan for 3 minutes, flip, then bake them for 2 minutes, or until nicely puffed up. Remove them from the oven and transfer them to a cooling rack for 5 to 10 minutes. Place the pitas in a basket and cover them with a dry towel to keep them soft while you bake the rest. Once all the pitas are ready, serve immediately or store at room temperature wrapped in a towel in a ziplock bag.

FLUFFY ROZ BEL SHA'ARIYA (RICE WITH VERMICELLI)

As with many world cuisines, most Middle Eastern meals come with a side of rice. Plain white rice is served sometimes, but vermicelli rice is far more common. There is a good reason for this: The toasted vermicelli adds a lovely, nutty savoriness to complement the mildness of the fluffy rice, while the butter adds a needed hint of richness. Often as a teenager, I was happy to eat a bowl of freshly cooked roz bel sha'ariya on its own because it's that good. If you can't find vermicelli, substitute it with fideo pasta.

YIELD: 3 TO 4 SERVINGS

1½ cups (300 g) long-grain white rice

1 tbsp (15 g) vegan butter or (15 ml) neutral oil

⅓ cup (35 g) short vermicelli (sha'ariya)

1 tsp sea salt

Place the rice in a fine-mesh sieve and rinse it in cold water. Wash the rice until the water runs clear, stirring it with your hands. Place the sieve over a large bowl and let the rice dry for 10 to 15 minutes.

In a medium pot, melt the butter over medium heat. Once bubbling, add the vermicelli and stir constantly until the vermicelli is toasted and golden, about 2 minutes. Watch it closely as it can burn easily. Add the rice and continue stirring for 30 seconds, then immediately add 3 cups (720 ml) of water and the salt. Cover the pot.

Turn the heat to high to bring it to a boil. Once boiling, turn the heat down to low so that the rice is gently simmering. Let it cook covered and undisturbed until all the water has been absorbed, 15 to 20 minutes.

Remove it from the heat and let it sit covered for at least 10 minutes. Once ready, fluff the vermicelli rice with a fork and serve it warm.

FRESH SALATA KHADRA (LOADED GREEN SALAD)

At most Middle Eastern tables—whether for breakfast, lunch or dinner—you'll find salata khadra or green salad, which is simply a raw vegetable salad prepared using whatever produce you have on hand and lightly dressed. I like to think of it as a slightly more sophisticated version of an American side salad. The mainstays of salata khadra are tomatoes, cucumbers and lime juice, but if my mom had been to the farmers' market or was entertaining for lunch, she would load it up with every color of the rainbow. This is a tradition I've carried with me, and we love salad in my household. Unlike the typical Egyptian version, I like to pack my salata khadra with a variety of fresh herbs and dress it with lime juice and olive oil. Throw in some chickpeas or lentils along with a loaf of pita and have a quick meal, or serve it alongside just about any dish for a pop of freshness.

YIELD: 4 SERVINGS

1 head romaine lettuce, chopped

¼ small head red cabbage, finely chopped

1 large carrot, grated

1 cup (149 g) cherry tomatoes, halved

½ English cucumber, chopped

1 yellow bell pepper, chopped

1 shallot, chopped

4–5 radishes, chopped

¼ cup (4 g) chopped fresh cilantro

¼ cup (15 g) chopped fresh parsley

1 tbsp (3 g) dill fronds

1 tbsp (6 g) chopped mint leaves

1 tbsp (15 ml) extra virgin olive oil

3 tbsp (45 ml) lime juice

½ tsp black pepper

1 tsp sea salt

In a large bowl, add the lettuce, cabbage, carrot, tomatoes, cucumber, bell pepper, shallot, radishes, cilantro, parsley, dill, mint, oil, lime juice, black pepper and salt. Toss to combine.

Chill for at least 15 minutes before serving.

JUICY "CHICKEN"

I spent months—if not years—perfecting my seitan preparations, and at this point they're among my most treasured vegan basics recipes. This seitan comes in two versions: breasts and thighs. The difference is that the breasts are firmer, denser and better suited for sandwiches or roasts. The thighs are juicer, flakier and better suited for stews and stir-frys. This recipe makes twelve pieces: You can make all breasts, all thighs or a mix of each.

YIELD: 12 PIECES

1 (15.5-oz [439-g]) can white navy beans, undrained

1 (15.5-oz [439-g]) can chickpeas, undrained

1 (12-oz [340-g]) block firm or extra firm silken tofu, undrained

2 cubes no-chicken bouillon

½ cup (40 g) nutritional yeast

2 tbsp (35 g) white miso paste

2 tbsp (30 ml) neutral oil

1 tbsp (7 g) garlic powder

1 tbsp (7 g) onion powder

1 tbsp (8 g) dried Italian herbs

1 tsp white pepper (optional)

3⅓ cups (400 g) vital wheat gluten

Oil spray, to shape

In a food processor, combine ⅓ cup (80 ml) of water with the navy beans, chickpeas, tofu, bouillon, nutritional yeast, miso, oil, garlic powder, onion powder, Italian herbs and pepper (if using). Pulse it until completely smooth and creamy.

Place the vital wheat gluten in a large bowl, then pour in the bean-tofu mixture. Using your hands, mix everything together until an elastic dough forms.

Divide the dough into four equal portions. Taking one portion at a time, place it in the food processor and pulse it for 5 to 7 seconds. Don't overprocess, otherwise the texture will be tough.

Scoop the dough out of the processor and knead it by hand a couple of times. Divide it into three portions and roll them into balls. You should end up with twelve dough balls.

To make chicken breasts, take one dough ball at a time and flatten it into a disc shape. Spray it with oil on both sides and place it on a cutting board. Using a mallet, pound it to tenderize it until it is about ½ inch (1.3 cm) thick. Shape it until it resembles a chicken breast.

To make chicken thighs, take one dough ball at a time and place it on a cutting board. Pull it into a tube/log shape. Twist it a couple of times, then tie it into a pretzel-like knot.

Fill two large pots—at least 4-quart (4-L) capacity—halfway with water. Cover the pots and bring the water to a boil. Once they are boiling, uncover, lower the heat to a simmer and add half of the chicken breasts and/or thighs to each pot. Make sure all the pieces are fully submerged and not overcrowded. Let them cook for 1 hour, flipping the chicken halfway through and adding more hot water when needed to keep the chicken fully submerged.

Once it is done cooking, remove the chicken using a slotted spoon. Place it on a cutting board and discard the cooking water. Allow the chicken to cool for at least 30 minutes before shredding it, cooking it or using it in a recipe. Store any chicken you're not using within 5 days in ziplock bags and freeze for up to 2 months. Defrost it in the fridge overnight before using.

SUCCULENT "STEAK"

Much like the "chicken" version, this seitan "steak" recipe was a game changer for me. Depending on the recipe you use it in, it can have a melt-in-your-mouth tender texture or a delightfully springy, meaty texture. I usually make these in bulk and keep them on hand to add to stews, skillets, casseroles or sandwiches—and to use them in multiple recipes in this book.

YIELD: 8 TO 9 LARGE STEAKS

For the Seitan

2 (15.5-oz [439-g] each) cans chickpeas, undrained
2 cubes vegetable bouillon
½ cup (40 g) nutritional yeast
3 tbsp (45 ml) soy sauce
1 tbsp (10 g) beet powder (for color, optional)
1½ tbsp (10 g) garlic powder
1½ tbsp (10 g) onion powder
1 tbsp (9 g) smoked paprika
½ tbsp (7 g) black pepper
½ tbsp (8 g) ground sage
3 cups (360 g) vital wheat gluten
Oil spray, to shape

For the Basic Preparation

1 tbsp (15 ml) soy sauce
1 tsp tomato paste
1 tsp liquid smoke
1 seitan "steak"
1 tbsp (15 ml) neutral oil

To Serve

2 medium cloves garlic, roasted
Chopped fresh parsley

In a food processor, combine ¾ cup (180 ml) of water with the chickpeas, bouillon, nutritional yeast, soy sauce, beet powder (if using), garlic powder, onion powder, smoked paprika, pepper and sage. Pulse it until completely pulverized.

Place the vital wheat gluten in a large bowl and pour the chickpea mixture onto it. Mix it together by hand. Once a dough is formed, knead the dough by hand for 5 minutes or place it in a food processor and pulse at a medium speed for 30 to 60 seconds. The dough should be moist and stretchy.

Divide the dough into eight to nine portions. Taking one portion at a time, roll it into a ball and flatten it into a disk. Place it on a cutting board and lightly spray it with oil on both sides. Using a mallet, tenderize and shape it into a ¾-inch (2-cm)-thick steak. The steaks will expand as they cook.

Fill two large pots—at least 4-quart (4-L) capacity—halfway with water. Cover the pots and bring the water to a boil. Once they are boiling, uncover and lower the heat to a simmer. Add the steaks to both pots in a single layer, making sure they're fully submerged; don't stack them. You may need to cook in batches if you are using only one pot.

The steaks will float as they cook, so flip them once or twice to cook them evenly on both sides. Simmer the steaks until they increase in size and are meaty and succulent, 45 to 60 minutes per batch. The steaks should have no doughiness whatsoever.

Remove the steaks from the pot, pat them dry and let them cool to room temperature. When they are cooked, you can use them immediately or store them for up to 1 week in the fridge or for up to 2 months in the freezer. If frozen, let them thaw in the fridge overnight, then lightly pat them dry before using.

For the basic preparation, whisk together the soy sauce, tomato paste and liquid smoke in a container with an airtight lid that is large enough to hold your steak. Add the steak and cover it in the marinade on all sides.

Heat the oil in a medium skillet over medium heat. Once the oil is smoking lightly, remove the steak from the marinade and place it in the skillet. Sear the steak, brushing it with the leftover marinade as it cooks, until crispy on both sides, about 3 minutes per side.

Remove the steak from the skillet and let it rest for at least 5 minutes before slicing. Serve the steak with roasted garlic and parsley.

MAGNIFICENT MAINS

Middle Eastern culture is all about honoring guests, sharing and creating lavish spreads for gatherings. In fact, if you don't cook enough food to feed at least three times the number of people you've invited over, it could be taken as an offense. This is why many of the mains featured here, such as Kabsa (page 31) and Maqluba (page 51), are more on the labor-intensive side and have some-what extensive ingredient lists. I promise the recipes are worth it!

Many of the dishes in this chapter are ones that are most often cooked for special occasions such as weddings, the holy month of Ramadan, religious feasts and to celebrate births. I've had Mahshi Felfel and Warak Enab (page 37) at practically every single family lunch at my grandmother's house. Lunch is the main meal in the Middle East, as opposed to dinner in Western culture. Similarly, Maqluba (page 51) in Palestine, Kabsa (page 31) in the Arabian Peninsula, Kusksu (page 49) in Libya and Fatteh (page 33) in Lebanon are all celebratory dishes meant to be served on a massive platter and enjoyed with loved ones.

To balance things out, I've included a few relatively effortless, absolutely delicious recipes that are great for laid-back weeknight dinners such as Kebab Karaz (page 38), "Chicken" Mbakbaka (page 45) and Tofu Shakshuka (page 55). Every single dish in this section is guaranteed to wow your taste buds and take you on a captivating culinary journey through the Middle East.

KABSA (SPICED RICE PILAF WITH "CHICKEN" SOY CURLS)

Kabsa *is a rice dish that's popular across the Arabian Peninsula, and it is the national dish of Saudi Arabia. My family moved to Saudi Arabia when I was a year old, so some of my earliest food memories are of eating it. Usually presented on a giant platter as a centerpiece, it combines whole and powdered spices with rice and vegetables, and it is topped with succulent meat, nuts and herbs for a delectable feast. I used Butler Soy Curls™ as a chicken substitute, and it was a perfect fit. I also made a side of* daqoos, *a spicy tomato sauce traditionally served with kabsa. This is a wonderfully layered, scrumptious dish that is perfect for entertaining.*

YIELD: 8 TO 10 SERVINGS

For the Rice Pilaf

3 cups (537 g) basmati rice

¼ cup (60 ml) neutral oil, divided

1 large onion, finely chopped

1 medium leek, finely chopped

4 medium cloves garlic, minced

2 medium carrots, chopped

1 cinnamon stick

4 cardamom pods, punctured

2 bay leaves

3 tbsp (48 g) plus ½ tbsp (8 g) tomato paste, divided

3 medium Roma tomatoes, diced

1 red chile pepper, chopped

2 vegetable bouillon cubes, crumbled

2 tsp (10 g) sea salt, divided

1 (8-oz [227-g]) bag Butler Soy Curls, rehydrated then drained

For the Kabsa Spices

2 tsp (8 g) loomi (limu omani/dried black lime powder)

1 tsp smoked paprika

1 tsp ground cinnamon

1 tsp ground cumin

1 tsp ground coriander

1 tsp Lebanese 7 Spice (page 45)

1 tsp ground turmeric

½ tsp ground cardamom

Place the rice in a fine-mesh strainer and thoroughly rinse it for a few minutes. Place the strainer on top of a large bowl and let the rice dry for at least 15 minutes.

To make the kabsa spices, add the loomi, paprika, cinnamon, cumin, coriander, 7 spice, turmeric and cardamom to a small bowl. Stir to combine, then set aside 2 teaspoons (7 g) of the mixture in a separate bowl.

To make the rice pilaf, heat 2 tablespoons (30 ml) of neutral oil in a large pot over medium-low heat. Once shimmery, add the onion and leek. Cook, stirring occasionally, until softened and golden, about 15 minutes. Add the garlic and carrots and cook until the garlic is fragrant, 1 to 2 minutes. Add the cinnamon, cardamom and bay leaves and toast for 1 minute.

Add all the kabsa spices, except the 2 teaspoons (7 g) you set aside. Mix well for 30 seconds. Add 3 tablespoons (48 g) of the tomato paste and, using a spatula, stir until the tomato paste has softened and is well incorporated. Add the tomatoes and chile pepper and cook, stirring occasionally, until the tomatoes have broken down, about 5 minutes.

Add the bouillon cubes, 1 teaspoon of salt and 6¼ cups (1.5 L) of water. Cover the pot and turn the heat to high. Once boiling, reduce the heat to low and ladle out about ¼ cup (60 ml) of the mixture and set it aside. Stir the basmati rice into the pot, cover it and simmer until all the liquid has been absorbed and the rice is tender, 15 to 20 minutes. Remove the pot from the heat, keep it covered and set it aside.

While the rice cooks, add the ¼ cup (60 ml) of reserved kabsa broth and the remaining ½ tablespoon (8 g) of tomato paste to a small bowl. Stir until well incorporated. Set it aside.

In a large skillet, heat the remaining 2 tablespoons (30 ml) of neutral oil over medium heat. Once shimmery, add the soy curls and the kabsa broth mixture. Stir it vigorously to coat all the soy curls. Continue cooking, stirring occasionally, until the curls begin to crisp up, about 5 minutes. Add the reserved 2 teaspoons (7 g) of kabsa spices and 1 teaspoon of salt. Continue cooking until the curls are golden and crispy, 8 to 9 minutes. Remove the skillet from the heat and set it aside.

(continued)

For the Daqoos Sauce

5 medium Roma tomatoes, quartered

4 mini sweet red bell peppers, seeded and halved

1 red chile pepper

1 tbsp (15 ml) neutral oil

2 medium cloves garlic, minced

3 tbsp (45 ml) white vinegar

3 tbsp (48 g) tomato paste

1 tsp smoked paprika

1 tsp sea salt

To Serve

Chopped fresh parsley

Raisins of choice

Pine nuts

Chopped pistachios

Red pepper flakes

To make the sauce, add the tomatoes, bell peppers and chile pepper to a blender. Pulse it until completely smooth. Set it aside. In a medium saucepan, heat the oil over medium-low heat. Once shimmery, add the garlic and cook, stirring, until fragrant and lightly golden, about 2 minutes. Add the vinegar and stir for 1 minute. Add the tomato paste and smoked paprika. Cook, stirring occasionally, for 2 minutes. Add the blended tomato mixture and salt, stir to combine and let the sauce simmer for 10 minutes. Remove it from the heat and set it aside.

Gently fluff the kabsa with a fork and discard the whole spices and bay leaf before plating. Top the kabsa with the crispy soy curls, parsley, raisins, pine nuts, pistachios and red pepper flakes. Serve with the daqoos sauce on the side.

MIXED MUSHROOM FATTEH (TOASTED PITA BREAD WITH TAHINI YOGURT, CHICKPEAS AND SAUCY MUSHROOM "MEAT")

Fatteh means "to break" or "broken." Here it refers to the chief ingredient: chopped up toasted pita bread. There are many variations, and this one is Levantine-style. The recipe was inspired by cookbook author Reem Kassis's version, but mine is vegan. I also added sun-dried tomatoes and leeks to further enhance the umami of the dish. My husband described the dish as Middle Eastern nachos and, while I don't recommend you try to eat this by hand, I think it's an apt enough description. The crispy pita bread is loaded with a rich, meaty and zesty mushroom layer. Then it is topped with a cool, refreshing yogurt sauce and sprinkled with dill, spices and almonds for freshness and extra crunch.

YIELD: 4 TO 5 SERVINGS

For the Bread

3–4 medium loaves The Best Pita Bread (page 19), cut into 1-inch (2.5-cm) squares

For the Yogurt Sauce

1½ cups (232 g) vegan yogurt

3 tbsp (45 g) tahini

3 tbsp (45 ml) lemon juice

1 tsp garlic powder

½ tsp white pepper (optional)

½ tsp sea salt

For the Mushrooms

2 oz (57 g) vegan butter

1 tbsp (15 ml) olive oil

1 large leek, thoroughly cleaned and chopped

2 medium shallots, finely chopped

3 medium cloves garlic, minced

10 oz (283 g) shiitake mushrooms, chopped

10 oz (283 g) cremini mushrooms, chopped

6 oz (170 g) portobello mushrooms, chopped

2 tsp (10 g) sea salt

Preheat the oven to 350°F (180°C) and line a baking sheet with parchment paper. Spread the pita bread in an even layer on the baking sheet. Bake until lightly golden and crispy, about 10 minutes. This could take less time depending on your oven; check it regularly. Set the pita aside.

To make the sauce, add the yogurt, tahini, lemon juice, garlic powder, white pepper (if using) and salt to a container with an airtight lid. Mix until all the ingredients are fully incorporated, then refrigerate until the rest of the components are ready.

To make the mushrooms, combine the butter and olive oil in a large pan or skillet over medium heat. Once bubbling, add the leek and shallots and cook until starting to turn golden at the edges, about 3 minutes. Add the garlic and cook, stirring to avoid burning, until fragrant, about 1 minute.

Add the shiitake, cremini and portobello mushrooms. Sprinkle them with salt and mix well. Reduce the heat to medium-low and cook until most of the moisture released by the mushrooms has evaporated and the mushrooms are softened and meaty, about 12 minutes.

(continued)

MIXED MUSHROOM FATTEH (TOASTED PITA BREAD WITH TAHINI YOGURT, CHICKPEAS AND SAUCY MUSHROOM "MEAT") (CONT.)

1½ cups (246 g) cooked chickpeas

⅓ cup (60 g) jarred sun-dried tomatoes, chopped (marinated in olive oil)

2 tbsp (40 g) pomegranate molasses

1 tbsp (15 ml) maple syrup

To Serve

1 tsp neutral oil

2 oz (57 g) white beech mushrooms

2 tbsp (13 g) dill fronds

⅓ cup (36 g) slivered almonds

1 tsp sumac

1 tsp Aleppo pepper

Add the chickpeas and sun-dried tomatoes, mix and cook for 1 minute, or until the chickpeas are warmed. Add the pomegranate molasses and maple syrup, mix and cook for 2 minutes to lightly caramelize. Remove the pan from the heat and set it aside.

To prepare the white beech mushroom topping for serving, heat the neutral oil in a small pan over medium-low heat. Once shimmery, add the white beech mushrooms and cook, stirring regularly, until softened and lightly golden, 2 to 3 minutes. Set them aside.

To assemble, lay the pita bread chips in an even layer on a large platter. Add the mushroom mixture, making sure to mostly cover the bread. Spoon the sauce on top, then sprinkle with the white beech mushrooms, dill, slivered almonds, sumac and Aleppo pepper. Serve immediately to avoid the bread getting soggy.

MAHSHI FELFEL AND WARAK ENAB (STUFFED BELL PEPPERS AND GRAPEVINE LEAVES)

When I first moved to the United States, mahshi *was the dish I was most nostalgic for and the first thing I'd request on trips back home. It took me many attempts to master my mother's recipe for this dish well enough to earn the approval of Middle Eastern aunties with exacting standards, but it was well worth it. Every single ingredient in the stuffing, from the herbs to the juicy tomatoes to the spices, lends a distinctive note to the finished dish, and each bite is a clear representation of Middle Eastern cuisine. This specific version of mahshi is Egyptian, though it borrows sumac from Levantine versions. The preparation of stuffed grapevine leaves and peppers is traditional and for good reason: The briny leafy flavor of the grapevine is offset beautifully by the mellow, slightly sweet peppers.*

YIELD: 6 TO 8 SERVINGS

1½ lb (680 g) Roma tomatoes

2 tbsp (32 g) tomato paste

1½ tsp (6 g) ground cumin

1½ tsp (6 g) ground coriander

1½ tsp (6 g) sumac

½ tsp ground cinnamon

¼ tsp ground allspice

¼ tsp ground nutmeg

¼ tsp ground cardamom

2 tsp (10 g) sea salt

3 cups (600 g) long-grain white rice, soaked in warm water for 30 minutes then rinsed

2 medium yellow onions, grated

2 cups (104 g) dill, finely chopped

1 cup (60 g) parsley, finely chopped

1 tightly packed cup (30 g) cilantro, finely chopped

40 grapevine leaves

7 large bell peppers, seeded

3–4 cups (720–960 ml) vegetable broth

To Serve

Cilantro leaves

Lime wedges

1–2 pickled chile peppers

In a food processor, combine the tomatoes, tomato paste, cumin, coriander, sumac, cinnamon, allspice, nutmeg, cardamom and salt. Pulse it until smooth. Transfer the mixture to a large bowl along with the rice, onions, dill, parsley and cilantro. Mix well.

To stuff the grapevine leaves, take one leaf at a time, place about a teaspoon of the rice filling, fold the sides and roll it tightly into a cylindrical shape.

To stuff the peppers, simply fill them three-quarters of the way full; this leaves room for the rice to expand as it cooks without spilling over. You could use the pepper tops or discard them. I opted to use mine.

To cook, stack the stuffed leaves and arrange the peppers in a large pot. Add the broth. The broth should only fill three-quarters of the pot; it should remain at a lower level than the tops of the stuffed peppers and shouldn't spill into them.

Cover the pot and place it over high heat. Once boiling, reduce the heat to a simmer. Cover the pot and cook for 30 to 35 minutes, or until the rice is tender and fluffy and the peppers and vine leaves are soft, but not mushy.

Remove the pot from the heat and let it sit covered for 5 to 10 minutes. Serve immediately garnished with a few cilantro leaves and with lime wedges and pickled chile peppers on the side.

KEBAB KARAZ ("MEATBALLS" IN SOUR CHERRY SAUCE)

Kebab karaz is a Syrian dish that features lamb meatballs in a sour cherry sauce. To mimic the richness of the lamb kebabs in this recipe, I created a vegan meatball out of cremini mushrooms, black beans, walnuts and bulgur wheat. Each ingredient adds a distinctive layer of texture and flavor that, when combined, produces a vegan kebab that holds its shape, is substantial without being dense and is delectably savory. The umami of the kebabs is balanced by the fruity, tangy and slightly sweet cherry sauce, resulting in a very memorable dish.

YIELD: 2 TO 3 SERVINGS

For the Kebabs

1 tbsp (15 ml) neutral oil

1 medium yellow onion, chopped

16 oz (455 g) cremini mushrooms, chopped

1 tsp ground coriander

1 tsp smoked paprika

1 tsp sea salt

Few pumps nonstick oil spray

8 oz (227 g) walnuts, toasted then cooled

1½ cups (260 g) cooked black beans

1 cup (180 g) cooked bulgur

For the Karaz Sauce

12 oz (340 g) pitted sour cherries

2 tbsp (30 g) sugar

1 tbsp (20 g) pomegranate molasses

1 tsp black pepper

1 tsp sea salt

½ tsp ground nutmeg

½ tsp ground allspice

To Serve

1 tbsp (4 g) chopped fresh parsley

1–2 tbsp (9–18 g) chopped almonds

The Best Pita Bread (page 19), toasted

To make the kebabs, heat the oil in a heavy bottom skillet over medium heat. Once shimmery, add the onion and mushrooms. Cook, stirring occasionally, until most of the moisture released by the mushrooms has evaporated and the onion has softened, 10 to 12 minutes. Stir in the coriander, paprika and salt. Cook for 2 minutes, or until well incorporated and fragrant. Set it aside and let it cool to room temperature.

Preheat the oven to 400°F (205°C) and grease a sheet pan with nonstick oil spray.

Place the walnuts in a food processor and pulse into crumbles, then add in the black beans, bulgur and onion-mushroom mixture. Pulse it until it is broken down enough that the dough easily holds together when shaped, but avoid overprocessing.

Using damp hands, shape the dough into 10 to 12 balls and place them on the sheet pan. Spray the balls with oil. Bake them until crispy on the outside, 20 to 25 minutes. The kebabs will firm up as they cool.

To make the sauce, add 1 cup (240 ml) of water to a medium pot. Add the cherries, sugar, pomegranate molasses, black pepper, salt, nutmeg and allspice. Stir to combine. Bring to a boil, then lower to a simmer. Cook uncovered until the sauce is reduced by half and has a jam-like consistency, about 20 minutes. Remove the pot from the heat.

Gently roll the kebabs in the cherry sauce to coat them. Serve the kebabs warm, topped with parsley and almonds and with a side of toasted pita bread.

BABY POTATO AND JACKFRUIT TAGINE

The classic Moroccan chicken tagine falls somewhere between being a stew and a curry. This vegetable-forward version is hearty, thanks to the warm spices in the Ras el Hanout, but it's also very fresh and zesty, thanks to the olives and preserved lemons. As a substitute for chicken, I chose jackfruit for its meatiness and baby potatoes for their creaminess. I also added dried apricots, a staple in Moroccan cuisine, but not typically used in this recipe, for a hint of sweetness.

YIELD: 6 SERVINGS

For the Tagine

4 medium cloves garlic, peeled

2 medium shallots, peeled and halved

2 tbsp (12 g) grated fresh ginger

1 cup (8 g) fresh cilantro, leaves and stems

1½ tbsp (12 g) Ras el Hanout (see Note)

½ tsp saffron

3 tbsp (45 ml) extra virgin olive oil

2 (20-oz [585-g]) cans young green jackfruit in brine, drained then sliced into thin strips

1½ lb (680 g) baby potatoes, halved

2 medium preserved lemons, pulp removed and rind thinly sliced

12 medium kalamata olives, pitted and halved

10 medium green olives, pitted and halved

¼ cup (48 g) dried apricots, thinly sliced

1 tsp sea salt

½ tsp white pepper (optional)

2 tbsp (30 ml) lemon juice

To Serve

Pomegranate arils

Chopped fresh parsley

Cooked couscous or other cooked grain

The Best Pita Bread (page 19)

In a food processor, combine the garlic, shallots, ginger, cilantro, Ras el Hanout and saffron. Pulse it a few times, until finely chopped, but not pureed. The mixture should be coarse.

Heat the olive oil in a tagine or a heavy bottomed pan over medium-low heat. Once the oil is shimmery and crackling, add the mixture and fry, stirring it every now and then to prevent sticking, for 2 to 3 minutes, or until the garlic is lightly golden.

Add the jackfruit and baby potatoes and continue cooking for 5 minutes, stirring occasionally, until lightly golden at the edges. Add 1¼ cups (295 ml) of water and stir, making sure to scrape any brown bits on the bottom of the pan.

Add the preserved lemons, olives and apricots. Stir, cover, turn the heat to high and bring to a boil. Reduce the heat to low and simmer for 15 to 20 minutes, or until most of the water has been absorbed and the potatoes are fork tender.

Add the salt and pepper (if using), mix well and cook for 1 minute. Remove the tagine from the heat and stir in the lemon juice. Serve topped with pomegranate arils and parsley with a side of couscous and/or pita bread.

NOTE: If you don't have Ras el Hanout on hand, substitute with 1 teaspoon of ground coriander, ½ teaspoon ground turmeric, ½ teaspoon ground cinnamon, ½ teaspoon ground nutmeg, ½ teaspoon black pepper, ¼ teaspoon ground turmeric, ¼ teaspoon ground cardamom and ¼ teaspoon ground cloves.

MUSHROOM TURLI (TIAN PROVENÇAL)

Turli is a dish that somehow found a home in Egyptian cuisine despite being Albanian in origin, and it's one that's often regarded as simple at best. I kept the foundational ingredients and gave it an extensive makeover to transform it from understated to impressive. The outer ring of the turli was inspired by the French tian Provençal. The center echoes traditional turli presentation-wise, but has added pops of flavor thanks to harissa and pomegranate molasses. I also used shiitake and trumpet mushrooms for maximum umami. This is a cozy, yet light and bright, dish that is perfect for summertime.

YIELD: 3 TO 4 SERVINGS

For the Sauce
1 (25-oz [710-g]) jar marinara sauce of choice

2 tbsp (15 g) harissa paste

½ tbsp (10 g) pomegranate molasses

For the Outer Ring (see Note)
2 medium Japanese eggplants, sliced into rounds

1 tbsp (15 g) sea salt

2–3 medium zucchini, sliced into rounds

2–3 medium yellow squash, sliced into rounds

2–3 medium king oyster (trumpet) mushrooms, sliced into rounds

3–4 small Roma tomatoes, sliced into rounds

1 tbsp (15 ml) neutral oil

1 tsp sea salt

For the Center
1 tbsp (15 ml) neutral oil

1 medium yellow onion, chopped

1 cup (145 g) shiitake mushrooms, sliced

1 cup (110 g) green beans, trimmed and chopped

1 tsp sea salt

To Serve
Chopped fresh parsley

Chopped fresh basil

Slivered almonds

To make the sauce, add the marinara, harissa and pomegranate molasses to a medium bowl. Mix until thoroughly combined. Set it aside.

To prep the eggplant, lay the eggplant slices on a kitchen towel and sprinkle them with salt on both sides. Let them sit for 15 to 20 minutes, then gently press down each slice with a paper towel to release excess moisture and prevent sponginess. Set them aside.

To make the center, heat the oil in a large pot over medium heat. Once shimmery, add the onion and cook for 5 minutes, or until lightly golden at the edges. Add the shiitake mushrooms, green beans and salt. Mix everything together, cover the pot and lower the heat to medium-low. Cook, stirring occasionally, until the beans are tender and the mushrooms are crispy, 15 to 20 minutes. Remove the pot from the heat and stir in one-quarter of the sauce. Set it aside.

Preheat the oven to 400°F (205°C).

Spread the remaining sauce on the bottom of a large cast-iron skillet. To make the outer ring, arrange the sliced eggplant, zucchini, yellow squash, king oyster mushrooms and Roma tomatoes in an alternating pattern. Place the shiitake mixture in the center. Brush the outer ring of veggies with oil and sprinkle it with the salt.

Bake the turli for 30 to 40 minutes, or until the eggplant and zucchini are softened and crispy at the edges. Serve topped with parsley, basil and almonds.

N O T E : Use any variety of eggplant you have access to so long as it's similar in circumference to the rest of the vegetables. I recommend using a mandolin for slicing the veggies to save time and ensure even thickness.

"CHICKEN" MBAKBAKA (PASTA IN SPICY BROTHY TOMATO SAUCE)

Mbakbaka is perhaps the most quintessential of Libyan dishes. It is named after the bak-bak sound the tomato dish makes as it simmers. This one-pot wonder heroes pasta in a delectably rich and spicy tomato sauce that's both homey and refined. Mbakbaka typically features either chicken or lamb, but for this vegan version I've found that homemade seitan "chicken" thighs work best. Crispy tofu and/or chickpeas are also great options.

YIELD: 6 SERVINGS

For the Mbakbaka

3 tbsp (45 ml) olive oil

2 medium yellow onions, chopped

3 Juicy "Chicken" thighs (page 24), torn into large chunks

3 medium cloves garlic, minced

2–3 serrano peppers, chopped

1–2 jalapeños, chopped

1 medium green bell pepper, chopped

1 medium red bell pepper, chopped

1 tbsp (12 g) Lebanese 7 Spice (see Note)

1 tsp ground caraway

1 tsp ground turmeric

1 tbsp (15 g) sea salt

6 oz (170 g) tomato paste

1 (28-oz [794 g]) can crushed tomatoes

10 oz (⅔ box [284 g]) elbow pasta or another small shell variety

To Serve

Chopped fresh cilantro

Lime wedges

Fresh Salata Khadra (page 23) or any green salad

Heat the oil in a Dutch oven or a heavy bottomed pot over medium heat. Once shimmery, add the onions and cook for 2 minutes, until lightly golden at the edges. Add the chicken and cook until golden, about 10 minutes.

Add the garlic and all the peppers and cook until the garlic is fragrant, 2 to 3 minutes. Add the 7 spice, caraway, turmeric and salt. Stir for 1 minute to coat the chicken and all the veggies.

Add the tomato paste and stir for 1 minute to coat everything, then add the crushed tomatoes and 4 cups (960 ml) of water. Cover the pot, turn the heat to high and bring to a boil.

Once boiling, lower the heat to medium-low, stir in the pasta and simmer until the pasta is cooked and the tomato sauce has thickened. The mbakbaka should be a little runny—thinner than chili, but thicker than broth. Remove the pot from the heat. Plate the mbakbaka immediately topped with a little cilantro, garnished with lime wedges and served with a side salad.

NOTE: If you don't have 7 spice, combine 1 teaspoon of ground coriander, 1 teaspoon of ground cumin, 1 teaspoon of ground paprika, ½ teaspoon of ground nutmeg, ½ teaspoon of ground cloves, ½ teaspoon of ground cinnamon and ¼ teaspoon of ground cardamom in a small bowl. Store any leftovers in a spice jar with an airtight lid for up to 2 months.

MTEWEM ("MEATBALLS" AND CHICKPEA GARLIC TAGINE)

Roughly translated mtewem *means "garlicky" or "with garlic." This Algerian tagine typically features meat two ways: in chunks and ground up into meatballs. The meat is cooked in a thick, spicy red sauce with chickpeas and—you guessed it—lots of garlic. The sauce is the heart of this dish, and I chose to give it my full attention in this recipe. That's why I used—and recommend using—store-bought vegan meat products in this recipe.*

YIELD: 3 TO 4 SERVINGS

For the Mtewem

1 tbsp (15 ml) neutral oil

1 large onion, chopped

6–7 medium cloves garlic, minced

8 oz (227 g) vegan grounds (I used Morningstar Farms® Starters Grillers Veggie Crumbles)

1 tsp ground cumin

1 tsp ground cinnamon

1 tsp smoked paprika

1 tsp red pepper flakes

1 tsp sea salt

2 tbsp (32 g) tomato paste

1 tbsp (8 g) chickpea flour dissolved in ½ cup (120 ml) cold water

1½ cups (246 g) cooked chickpeas

¾ cup (101 g) frozen green peas

1 (12.7-oz [360-g]) package vegan meatballs (I used Gardein® Classic Meatless Meatballs.)

To Serve

Chopped fresh parsley

1 small serrano pepper, chopped

Cooked basmati rice

Lime wedges

Heat the oil over medium heat in a tagine or heavy bottomed pan. Once shimmery, add the onion and cook until softened and lightly golden, about 8 minutes. Stir in the garlic and cook until fragrant, about 2 minutes. Add the grounds and cook, stirring occasionally, until golden and crispy, about 10 minutes.

Add the cumin, cinnamon, smoked paprika, red pepper flakes and salt. Stir for 30 seconds. Add the tomato paste, then stir to break apart and lightly cook for 1 minute. Add the chickpea flour slurry, chickpeas, peas and meatballs along with 2 cups (480 ml) of water.

Cover and turn the heat to high to bring to a boil. Lower the heat to a simmer and cook until the meatballs are tender and juicy and the sauce has thickened, 15 to 20 minutes. Remove the pot from the heat. Serve immediately topped with parsley and serrano peppers with a side of rice and a couple of lime wedges.

KUSKSU BEL KHALTA (COUSCOUS AND VEGGIES IN SPICY SAUCE WITH CRISPY TOPPING)

Kusksu is a traditional Libyan dish that pairs fluffy couscous with a stew made of potatoes, pumpkin, chickpeas and beef in a spicy hararat *(Libyan 5 spice) sauce. For my take on this recipe, I omitted the beef. Instead, I opted to top the kusksu with* khalta, *which is typically a mix of liver; I used tempeh, the closest in texture as far as vegan alternatives go. I also included toasted nuts and dried fruit most commonly used in Egyptian rice pilaf, along with delicata and honeynut squash to further jazz up the dish. This recipe truly is an explosion of flavors, and it's a perfect representation of the richness of Libyan cuisine.*

YIELD: 6 SERVINGS

For the Stew

2 tbsp (30 ml) olive oil

1 large onion, chopped

2 medium Yukon gold potatoes, cubed

1 small honeynut or butternut squash, peeled and seeded then cubed

1 small delicata squash, seeded then cubed

2 medium Roma tomatoes, chopped

2 tbsp (32 g) tomato paste

1 tbsp (8 g) Hararat Spice Mix (see Note [page 50])

1 tsp ground turmeric

1 tsp sea salt

1 cube vegetable bouillon

1½ cups (246 g) cooked chickpeas

¾ cup (101 g) frozen green peas

For the Couscous

1 cube vegetable bouillon

1½ cups (260 g) couscous

1 tbsp (15 ml) extra virgin olive oil

Heat the olive oil in a Dutch oven or thick bottomed pot. Once shimmery, add the onion and cook until slightly softened and translucent, about 5 minutes. Add the potatoes and continue cooking, stirring occasionally, for 7 minutes, or until slightly softened. Add the honeynut and delicata squash and cook for 5 minutes, or until slightly softened. Add the tomatoes and cook until broken down, 3 to 4 minutes.

Add the tomato paste and use a spatula to break it apart for 1 to 2 minutes. Stir in the Hararat Spice Mix, turmeric and salt for about 30 seconds. Add the vegetable bouillon, chickpeas and peas along with 2½ cups (590 ml) of water. Turn the heat to high to bring it to a boil. Reduce the heat to a simmer, cover and cook, stirring occasionally, until the potatoes and squash are tender, 12 to 15 minutes. Remove the pot from the heat.

To make the couscous, combine 2 cups (480 ml) of water and the vegetable bouillon in a large pot and bring to a boil. Add the couscous and extra virgin olive oil, mix well and remove it from the heat. Let it sit covered for at least 10 minutes. Fluff the couscous with a fork before serving.

(continued)

KUSKSU BEL KHALTA (COUSCOUS AND VEGGIES IN SPICY SAUCE WITH CRISPY TOPPING) (CONT.)

For the Khalta Topping

1 tbsp (14 g) vegan butter

1 (8-oz [227-g]) block tempeh, chopped into small triangles

¼ cup (35 g) raisins

3 tbsp (27 g) pumpkin seeds

2 tbsp (28 g) chopped walnuts

2 tbsp (14 g) slivered almonds

1 tsp sea salt

1 tsp blossom water

Cilantro microgreens or chopped fresh cilantro, to serve

To make the topping, melt the vegan butter in a skillet over medium heat. Once bubbling, add the tempeh. Cook, stirring occasionally, until golden and toasty, about 10 minutes. Add the raisins, pumpkin seeds, walnuts, almonds and salt. Cook until the nuts are fragrant and lightly toasted, 3 to 4 minutes. Remove the skillet from the heat, stir in the blossom water and set it aside.

To serve, start with a base layer of couscous, add the stew and top with the khalta and cilantro.

NOTE: If you don't have hararat, mix together 1½ teaspoons (7 g) of ground cinnamon, 1 teaspoon of ground cumin, 1 teaspoon of ground coriander, ½ teaspoon of ground allspice and ½ teaspoon of red pepper flakes in a small bowl. Store leftovers in a jar with an airtight lid for up to 2 months.

POTATO, EGGPLANT AND TOFU MAQLUBA (ONE-POT UPSIDE DOWN SPICED RICE)

Maqluba means "upside down", and this Levantine dish is made by laying fried vegetables, meat and rice in a pot. They are stewed together in a richly spiced broth then flipped onto a serving dish for an intricately layered showstopper. I combined tofu with creamy golden potatoes, earthy eggplant and warm Middle Eastern spices for an unforgettable culinary experience.

For the Maqluba

2 cups (400 g) long-grain white rice

2 medium eggplants, thinly sliced

1 tbsp (15 g) sea salt

¼ cup (60 ml) neutral oil, plus more as needed

3 medium Yukon gold potatoes, thinly sliced

1 medium red bell pepper, chopped

1 medium orange bell pepper, chopped

1 medium onion, chopped

½ tsp olive oil

2 medium zucchini, thinly sliced

11 oz (⅔ block [300 g]) super firm tofu, thinly sliced

4 cups (960 ml) vegetable broth

For the Spice Mix

1 tsp ground ginger

1 tsp ground cinnamon

1 tsp ground cumin

1 tsp ground coriander

1 tsp black pepper

1 tsp ground turmeric

½ tsp ground cardamom

2 tsp (10 g) sea salt

In a large bowl, combine the rice and 3 cups (720 ml) of hot water. Let the rice soak for 30 minutes, then drain it in a colander and set it aside.

Place the eggplant slices in a single layer on a kitchen towel. Sprinkle each slice with salt on both sides. Let them sit for at least 15 minutes. This allows excess moisture to be released, preventing a spongy texture.

In the meantime, heat ¼ cup (60 ml) of neutral oil in a skillet. Once lightly smoking, fry the potato slices in batches until golden on both sides, about 3 minutes per side. Place the potatoes on paper towels and set them aside.

Add 1 to 2 tablespoons (15 to 30 ml) of neutral oil to the skillet if needed before proceeding to fry the eggplant. Once ready, gently press each piece of eggplant with a paper towel to soak up the released moisture. Fry the eggplant until golden on both sides, about 2 minutes per side. Place the eggplant slices on paper towels and set them aside.

Wipe your skillet clean. Heat 1 tablespoon (15 ml) of neutral oil over medium heat. Once shimmery, add the bell peppers and onion. Cook, stirring occasionally, until they have softened, about 10 minutes. Remove the skillet from the heat and set it aside.

To make the spice mix, combine the ginger, cinnamon, cumin, coriander, black pepper, turmeric, cardamom and salt in a small bowl. Transfer the rice from the colander to a large bowl, add the spice mix and stir until well distributed.

To make the maqluba, grease the bottom and sides of a medium pot with the olive oil. Evenly cover the bottom with the sautéed peppers and onion. Add a layer of zucchini; press down the zucchini and be sure not to leave gaps at the edges. Add a layer of tofu, then a layer of the fried eggplant and then a layer of fried potatoes. Add the rice on top of the potatoes in an even layer. Gently pour in the vegetable broth, covering the rice by about 1 inch (2.5 cm).

(continued)

POTATO, EGGPLANT AND TOFU MAQLUBA
(ONE-POT UPSIDE DOWN SPICED RICE) (CONT.)

To Serve
Slivered almonds
Chopped fresh parsley

Cover the pot and place it over medium-high heat until it comes to a boil. Lower the heat to a simmer. Cover the pot with a towel and press the lid back on to trap in the heat and moisture. Make sure to fold up the edges of the towel to avoid a fire hazard. Cook for 30 minutes.

When the time is up, remove the pot from the heat, uncover and gently lift the towel. Place a large plate on top of the pot. Very carefully turn the pot upside down and place it on a flat surface. Let it sit for 15 minutes, then very gently lift up the pot. Avoid shaking it or removing it abruptly; this will keep your maqluba intact. Serve immediately topped with almonds and parsley.

TOFU SHAKSHUKA

Almost every region of the Middle East has its own version of shakshuka—eggs poached in a vibrant tomato sauce. The basic concept is the same in all the different localities; what varies are the secondary ingredients that go into the sauce. My recipe for shakshuka is closest to the Moroccan one and combines Ras el Hanout, harissa paste and sweet bell peppers with jammy tofu "eggs" for a multilayered and gorgeously savory flavor profile.

YIELD: 2 TO 3 SERVINGS

For the "Eggs"

10.5 oz (⅔ block [298 g]) super firm tofu

¼ cup (20 g) nutritional yeast

¾ cup (180 ml) unsweetened plant milk

1 tsp kala namak (see Note)

1 tsp garlic powder

1 tsp onion powder

1 tsp black pepper

½ tsp sea salt

¼ tsp ground turmeric

For the Shakshuka

2 tbsp (30 ml) neutral oil

1 medium onion, chopped

½ large red bell pepper, chopped

½ large yellow bell pepper, chopped

1 large green bell pepper, chopped

4 medium cloves garlic, minced

2 medium Roma tomatoes, chopped

1 tsp Ras el Hanout (page 41)

1 tsp smoked paprika

1 tsp ground cumin

1 tsp ground coriander

1 tsp sea salt

1 tbsp (15 g) harissa paste

16 oz (454 g) crushed tomatoes

To Serve

Vegan feta crumbles

Chopped fresh parsley

Sliced jalapeños

The Best Pita Bread (page 19), toasted

To prepare the "eggs," add the tofu, nutritional yeast, milk, kala namak, garlic powder, onion powder, black pepper, salt and turmeric to a food processor. Pulse it until smooth. Set it aside.

To make the shakshuka, heat the oil in a large skillet over medium heat. Once shimmery, add the onion and cook until translucent, about 3 minutes. Add all the bell peppers and continue cooking, stirring occasionally, until the vegetables have softened, about 10 minutes.

Add the garlic and cook, stirring to prevent burning, until fragrant, about 1 minute. Add the tomatoes, Ras el Hanout, smoked paprika, cumin, coriander and salt. Mix well and cook until the tomatoes have released their juice, about 10 minutes.

Add the harissa paste and mix until all the vegetables are well coated and the harissa is fragrant, about 1 minute. Add the crushed tomatoes. Turn the heat to high and bring to a boil, then reduce the heat to medium-low.

Using a spatula, create six to seven small wells in the sauce and, using an ice cream scoop, pour in your "eggs." I used 1½ scoops for each "egg." Cover and cook for 12 to 15 minutes, until the eggs are mostly firm to the touch; they will firm up more as they cool. Remove the the pan from the heat.

Serve warm topped with vegan feta, parsley and sliced jalapeños with a side of toasted pita.

N O T E : *Kala namak*, also called Himalayan black salt, is a type of salt that's naturally high in sulfur, which gives it a distinctive "eggy" smell and flavor. It is optimal for most vegan egg preparations. It is relatively inexpensive and can be easily found online; I order mine from Amazon.

TANTALIZING STREET FOOD

What I love about Middle Eastern street food is how accurately it captures the culinary pulse of the culture. Narrowing down the recipes for this chapter was difficult because of the sheer number of options. Ultimately, I selected the dishes I know most intimately which allowed me to maintain their authenticity.

Some of my favorite food memories are of weekly shawarma wrap dinners from a hole-in-the-wall Syrian shop near where I grew up in Saudi Arabia. Then there are the mini *hawawshis* purchased from rickety carts in downtown Cairo between college classes and the late-night visits to crowded *koshary* and *ta'amiya* stands packed with people from all walks of life. The recipes in this chapter are a combination of those memories and the cooking experience I've gained since.

Typically, Middle Eastern street food is humble and affordable, which is why a fair percentage of it is naturally vegan. It's also renowned for its bold flavors, abundance of spices and heat and overall greasy goodness. While many of the recipes can be eaten for whichever meal you prefer, Manakeesh Za'atar (page 63) are such an awesome breakfast/brunch option, while the Ta'amiya Bowls (page 67) make for a spectacular power-packed lunch. If you're looking for cozy vibes, the Mesaka'a (page 70) is definitely the way to go, while the Harissa Fried "Chicken" with Za'atar Fries (page 74) is a fun and flavorful choice if you're craving fast food, but fancier. No matter which recipe you choose to make first, I'm certain you'll love it!

KOSHARY (RICE, PASTA AND LEGUMES WITH FRIED ONIONS AND TOMATO-GARLIC SAUCE)

Koshary is the national dish of Egypt, and it just so happens to be vegan. Like many Egyptian street foods, it owes its popularity to its affordability and how easy it is to prepare. All the ingredients are common and inexpensive in Egypt: pasta, rice, chickpeas, lentils and super crispy onions. The dish is made with two sauces: a light vinegary daqqa, and a rich and robust sauce. It is best eaten when all the ingredients are mixed together while still warm. It can sound like an odd concoction at first, but it's one of the most delectable comfort meals there is. Whether homemade or bought from a hole-in-the-wall kiosk, koshary is the epitome of Middle Eastern soul food and is especially warming in colder months.

YIELD: 6 SERVINGS

For the Koshary

2 large onions, thinly sliced

¾ cup (180 ml) neutral oil

Pinch of sea salt

2 cups (372 g) cooked short-grain white rice

2 cups (396 g) cooked lentils

12 oz (340 g) elbow pasta, cooked according to package instructions

1½ cups (246 g) cooked chickpeas

Hot sauce, to serve (optional)

For the Tomato-Garlic Sauce

½ tbsp (8 ml) neutral oil

3 medium cloves garlic, minced

6 oz (170 g) tomato paste

1 tsp ground cumin

1 tsp cayenne

1 tsp sea salt

3 tbsp (45 ml) white vinegar

For the Daqqa

1 tbsp (15 ml) neutral oil

4 medium cloves garlic, minced

½ cup (120 ml) white vinegar

1 tbsp (7 g) ground coriander

½ tbsp (4 g) ground cumin

½ tsp sea salt

To prepare the onions, line a plate with paper towels. Heat the oil in a large skillet over medium heat. Once shimmery, add the onions and fry, stirring occasionally, until golden brown and crispy, about 12 minutes. Transfer the onions to the plate and sprinkle them with salt.

To make the sauce, heat the oil in a medium pot over medium heat. Once shimmery, add the garlic and cook until lightly golden, 1 to 2 minutes. Add the tomato paste and use a spatula to break it apart and lightly fry it for 1 to 2 minutes. Add 2 cups (480 ml) of water, cumin, cayenne and salt. Whisk together until the tomato paste is fully dissolved.

Turn the heat to high to bring the sauce to a boil. Lower to a simmer and cook for 10 minutes, or until it has thickened but is still easily pourable. Remove the pot from the heat, stir in the vinegar and set it aside.

To make the daqqa, heat the oil in a medium pot over medium-low heat. Once shimmery, add the garlic and cook it just long enough for the garlic to get fragrant; the garlic should still be white. Add the vinegar, coriander, cumin and salt along with ¾ cup (180 ml) of water. Stir and as soon as it starts boiling, remove it from the heat and set it aside.

Plate a base layer of rice, followed by a layer of lentils, then pasta, then chickpeas and finally top it with the crispy onions. Drizzle the koshary with a few spoonfuls of tomato sauce, and leave the rest on the side along with the daqqa and hot sauce. Serve it warm, and be sure to mix together all the layers and sauces for maximum flavor.

BEEF-STYLE SEITAN SHAWARMA WRAPS WITH TOUM (GARLIC DIP)

Shawarma wraps are the Middle Eastern equivalent of a burrito, but even more satisfying. While shawarma meat is traditionally made with stacked meat piled on a vertical stick, what really distinguishes it are the spices. I used juicy seitan "steaks" here, marinated and then cooked to crispy perfection. The seitan is paired with toum, *a Levantine garlic sauce that's similar to aioli but fluffier and yummier. This recipe is one of my most popular, and it's a true joy to eat.*

YIELD: 3 LARGE WRAPS

For the Toum

2 tbsp (15 g) cornstarch

5 medium cloves garlic, minced

1 tsp lime juice

½ tsp sea salt

6 tbsp (90 ml) vegetable oil

For the "Meat"

3 tbsp (45 ml) soy sauce

2 tbsp (25 g) Shawarma Seasoning (see Note)

1 tsp liquid smoke

2 large Succulent "Steaks" (page 27), cut into strips

2 tbsp (30 ml) neutral oil

For the Shawarma

1 batch toum

3 large flatbread loaves, such as lavash, warmed

Chopped lettuce or baby spinach

Chopped tomatoes

Sliced cucumbers

Sliced onions

To make the toum, combine the cornstarch with ¾ cup (180 ml) of water in a small saucepan over medium heat. Whisk together until bubbling and thickened, about 20 minutes. Let it cool to room temperature.

Combine the cornstarch mixture with the garlic, lime juice and salt in a blender. Pulse it until the garlic is completely pulverized, then add the vegetable oil 1 tablespoon (15 ml) at a time, pulsing between additions. Wait until the vegetable oil is fully incorporated before adding the next tablespoon. The mixture should start to emulsify by the third tablespoon; it will have a texture similar to mayonnaise and a bright white color. Set it aside.

To make the "meat," whisk together the soy sauce, Shawarma Seasoning and liquid smoke in a large bowl. Add the seitan strips and toss to coat. Refrigerate the "meat" for at least 1 hour.

To cook, line a plate with a paper towel. Heat the neutral oil in a large skillet over medium heat. Once shimmery, remove the seitan strips from the marinade and place them in the pan. Don't overcrowd. Cook each strip until it is crispy on all sides, 1 to 2 minutes per side. Transfer the seitan to the plate.

To serve the shawarma, spread 1 teaspoon of toum across slightly warmed flatbread, add all the vegetables, then top with the shawarma seitan and roll up. Top each wrap with more toum to taste and serve it immediately. Refrigerate any leftover toum for up to 5 days.

N O T E : If you don't have Shawarma Seasoning on hand, combine 1 tablespoon (7 g) of ground cumin, 1 tablespoon (7 g) of ground coriander, 1 tablespoon (9 g) of smoked paprika, 1 tablespoon (5 g) of ground ginger, 1 teaspoon of black pepper, 1 teaspoon of sumac, 1 teaspoon of Chinese five-spice powder, 1 teaspoon of ground cinnamon, ½ teaspoon of ground cardamom and ½ teaspoon of ground turmeric in a small bowl. Store the leftovers in a jar with an airtight lid for up to 2 months.

MANAKEESH ZA'ATAR (ZA'ATAR FLATBREAD)

In my high school, the canteen kiosk was run by Lebanese staff, and we'd have to hurry to get our hands on the freshly made and ridiculously tasty manakeesh *before they sold out. While there are various types of manakeesh, I chose to make za'atar ones because I think they're the tastiest and they're also naturally vegan. Think of manakeesh as breakfast flatbread pizzas. They're impossibly fluffy, and the simplicity of the topping allows the flavors of the individual za'atar constituents to shine: herbaceous wild thyme, zesty sumac and earthy sesame seeds. Manakeesh work great for just about any meal of the day. It can even be cut into slices and served as an appetizer.*

YIELD: 8 SERVINGS

For the Manakeesh

2½ tsp (10 g) active dry yeast

1 tbsp (15 g) sugar

2 tbsp (30 ml) olive oil, plus more for greasing

1 tsp baking powder

1 tsp sea salt

2 tbsp (15 g) vital wheat gluten (optional)

3 cups (375 g) all-purpose flour, plus more for dusting

For the Topping

¾ cup (180 ml) olive oil

½ cup (56 g) za'atar

In a large bowl, whisk together the yeast, sugar and 1 cup (240 ml) of warm water. Let it sit for 10 to 15 minutes, or until a layer of foam has formed, indicating the yeast is active. Add the olive oil, baking powder, salt and vital wheat gluten (if using) and whisk to combine. Add the flour, mixing it in by hand, then knead to combine. Transfer the dough to a floured surface and knead until it no longer sticks to your hands but remains moist and elastic, about 10 minutes.

Place the dough in a large clean bowl lightly greased with olive oil. Roll the dough in the bowl so that all sides are coated in oil, cover it with a damp towel and leave it in a warm, dark spot until it is doubled in size, about 1 hour.

Meanwhile, make the topping. In a medium bowl, mix together the olive oil and za'atar until well incorporated. Set it aside. Preheat the oven to 450°F (230°C) and lightly grease two large sheet pans with olive oil.

Once the dough has risen, divide into eight equal portions and roll each portion into a ball. Take one ball at a time—leaving the rest of the balls covered with a damp towel—and roll it out into a disc about 6 inches (15 cm) in diameter. Cover it with a damp cloth while you roll the rest. Place as many flatbreads as you can fit on the sheet pan without crowding them, keeping the rest covered until you're ready to bake.

Slather the flatbreads generously with the za'atar topping. Bake until the dough is fluffed up and golden at the edges and the bottom, 5 to 6 minutes per batch. Repeat the baking steps for the remaining flatbreads. Let them cool for about 5 minutes. Serve warm or at room temperature.

KEBAB SKEWERS (MARINATED LENTIL SEITAN "BEEF") WITH SALATET ZABADI (YOGURT DIP)

Every Middle Eastern region has at least one version of kebabs. The recipe I created here is a play on the Egyptian kebab, which is typically made from boneless beef sirloin rather than the ground beef used in almost all other variations. I use a combination of lentils, chickpeas and vital wheat gluten to craft succulent, tender chunks of "beef" that are immersed in a smoky marinade, skewered and roasted to savory perfection. I paired the kebab with a light and refreshing salatet zabadi *(yogurt dip/tzatziki) and served it with salad and quinoa.*

YIELD: 4 SERVINGS

For the Kebab Dough

1 (15-oz [425-g]) can lentils, undrained

⅔ cup (109 g) cooked chickpeas

3 tbsp (45 ml) soy sauce

2 tbsp (30 g) harissa paste

1 tbsp (12 g) mushroom seasoning or no-beef bouillon

2 tsp (10 ml) liquid smoke

1 tbsp (7 g) onion powder

1 tbsp (7 g) garlic powder

1 tbsp (7 g) smoked paprika

1 tsp dried sage

1 tsp sea salt

2 cups (240 g) vital wheat gluten, plus more if needed

For the Kebab Marinade

3 tbsp (45 ml) olive oil

2 tbsp (30 ml) soy sauce

1 tbsp (20 g) pomegranate molasses

1 tbsp (15 ml) liquid smoke

1 tsp smoked paprika

1 tsp ground coriander

To make the kebab, add 1 cup (240 ml) of water to a food processor with the lentils, chickpeas, soy sauce, harissa, mushroom seasoning, liquid smoke, onion powder, garlic powder, smoked paprika, sage and salt. Pulse it until completely smooth and creamy.

Place the vital wheat gluten in a large bowl. Pour the creamy lentil mixture on top and knead until combined. Add more gluten 1 tablespoon (8 g) at a time if the mixture is too wet and not holding together. Transfer the dough to a stand mixer with the dough hook attachment and knead for 5 minutes or knead by hand for 10 minutes. The dough should be elastic and moist without being crumbly.

Fill a large pot halfway with water and bring it to a boil, then lower the heat to a simmer. Chop the kebab dough into bite-sized pieces; smaller is better because seitan expands as it cooks. Transfer the seitan to the pot and simmer the seitan bites for 30 to 40 minutes, or until meaty and tender. Drain the seitan bites and set them aside to cool.

To make the marinade, whisk together the oil, soy sauce, pomegranate molasses, liquid smoke, smoked paprika and coriander in a large container with a lid. Transfer the seitan to the container and toss to coat. Refrigerate and let marinate for at least 4 hours or overnight.

To cook the kebab, preheat the oven to 400°F (205°C). Arrange the seitan bites on skewers, transfer them to a grilling pan, brush them with the marinade and roast them for 10 minutes. Flip the skewers, brush them with the marinade again and continue roasting until crispy on all sides, about 7 to 10 more minutes. Remove the pan from the oven and set it aside.

(continued)

KEBAB SKEWERS (MARINATED LENTIL SEITAN "BEEF") WITH SALATET ZABADI (YOGURT DIP) (CONT.)

For the Salatet Zabadi

1½ cups (115 g) vegan yogurt

1 English cucumber, grated then placed in a towel and wrung out

¼ cup (13 g) chopped dill

2 tbsp (11 g) chopped mint leaves

2 tbsp (30 ml) lemon juice

1 large clove garlic, minced

1 tsp sea salt

To Serve

Spring mix

Sliced cherry tomatoes

Sliced cucumbers

Chopped fresh mint

Pickled red onions

Cooked quinoa

Lime wedges

To make the salatet zabadi, combine the yogurt, cucumber, dill, mint, lemon juice, garlic and salt in a large container with an airtight lid. Mix well and cover. Refrigerate until ready to use or for up to 3 days.

To plate, start with a base of spring mix, then top with tomatoes, cucumbers, mint, pickled onions and the kebab skewers. Serve with a side of salatet zabadi, quinoa and a couple of lime wedges.

TA'AMIYA (FAVA BEAN FALAFEL) BOWLS WITH SPICY CUMIN TOMATOES

Ta'amiya is a type of falafel made from split fava beans and tons of greens. It's naturally vegan, unique to Egypt and one of its most popular street foods. Like Levantine chickpea falafel, ta'amiya has a delightfully crispy exterior, but the moist and fluffy interior is what makes it truly special. Though usually served in pita pockets, I made it the centerpiece of a nutritious feast of a bowl instead. To amp up the deliciousness, I included a side of my mom's simple, yet insanely addictive, spicy cumin tomatoes as well.

YIELD: ABOUT 20 TA'AMIYA/
4 SERVINGS TOMATO SALAD

For the Ta'amiya

1 cup (200 g) split fava beans

1 medium leek, white and light green parts only, roughly chopped

1 cup (50 g) scallions, roughly chopped

1 cup (25 g) fresh cilantro, tightly packed

½ cup (30 g) fresh parsley

¼ cup (12 g) fresh chives

3 medium cloves garlic, peeled

1 tsp ground coriander

1 tsp ground cumin

1 tsp cayenne (optional)

1 tsp sea salt

1 cup (240 ml) neutral oil, for frying

¼ cup (36 g) white sesame seeds

Place the split fava beans in a large bowl and cover them with water. Soak them overnight; they should double in size.

Rinse the beans well. To a food processor, add the beans, leek, scallions, cilantro, parsley, chives, garlic, coriander, cumin, cayenne (if using) and salt. Pulse it until the mixture is completely smooth, fluffy and vibrant green. Use immediately, refrigerate for up to 3 days or freeze in storage bags for up to 2 months. Thaw the mixture in the fridge overnight before using.

To cook the ta'amiya, heat the oil in a medium skillet on low heat; this prevents the ta'amiya from turning dark brown/black and not cooking in the middle. Using lightly dampened hands, scoop about a tablespoon (15 ml) of the batter and toss it to shape it into a ball. Gently flatten it into a small disc; it's completely normal for the dough to feel too wet and/or fluffy compared to chickpea falafel. Press a few sesame seeds in the center of each side of the disc.

Line a plate with a paper towel. Fry the ta'amiya until crispy and golden brown on both sides, about 2 minutes per side. Transfer them to the plate.

(continued)

TA'AMIYA (FAVA BEAN FALAFEL) BOWLS WITH
SPICY CUMIN TOMATOES (CONT.)

For the Tomato Salad

2 cups (298 g) cherry
tomatoes, sliced

1 tbsp (5 g) dried mint

3 tbsp (45 ml) lemon juice,
or more to taste

1 tsp ground cumin

½ tsp cayenne

½ tsp sea salt

To Serve

Spring mix

Fluffy cooked quinoa

Sliced onions

Pepperoncinis

Pitted kalamata olives, halved

Lemon wedges

Tahini sauce

To make the tomato salad, toss together the tomatoes, mint, lemon juice, cumin, cayenne and salt in a medium bowl. Refrigerate it until ready to use or for up to 4 hours.

Arrange all the components in a serving bowl. Serve the ta'amiya while it's still hot.

MESAKA'A (FRIED EGGPLANT AND POTATO MOUSSAKA)

Mesaka'a is a popular "peasant" Egyptian street food because the ingredients are quite inexpensive. It's typically eaten with a side of pita for gloriously sloppy dipping or as deliciously messy pita pockets. The eggplant, potatoes and chile peppers are fried until golden and crispy, then dunked in a chunky, deeply savory, garlic-tomato sauce. This is a family recipe that's been passed from my grandmother to my mom to me, and it is a wonderful representation of authentic Egyptian cuisine.

YIELD: 4 TO 5 SERVINGS

For the Mesaka'a

2 large eggplants, sliced into rounds

Sea salt for sprinkling the eggplant, plus 2 tsp (10 g) for the sauce, divided

4 medium Russet potatoes, peeled and cut into fries

¾ quart (710 ml) plus 1 tbsp (15 ml) neutral oil, divided

2 medium jalapeños, halved (leave seeds in for a spicier version or scrape them out for a milder one)

4 medium cloves garlic, minced

6 oz (170 g) tomato paste

1 (14.5-oz [411-g]) can fire-roasted diced tomatoes

¾ cup (183 g) crushed tomatoes

1 tsp ground cumin

1 tsp black pepper

½ tsp cayenne (optional)

1 tbsp (15 ml) white vinegar

To Serve

Chopped fresh parsley

The Best Pita Bread (page 19)

To prepare the eggplant, place the slices on a towel and sprinkle them with salt on both sides. Let them sit for at least 30 minutes. Using a paper towel, gently press down on each slice of eggplant to absorb the released moisture; the slices should significantly decrease in thickness. Set them aside.

Soak the fries in cold water for 15 to 20 minutes, then drain and dry them. Set them aside.

Divide ¾ quart (710 ml) of oil between two large skillets and heat them over medium heat. Once the oil is lightly smoking, fry the eggplant in batches in one skillet until crispy and golden, 8 to 10 minutes per batch. Set them aside.

Add the fries to the other skillet and fry them in batches until golden and crispy, 7 to 9 minutes per batch. Set them aside. In the same skillet used for the fries, add the jalapeños and fry them until the skin is slightly blistered and the flesh is golden at the edges. Set them aside.

To make the sauce, heat the remaining 1 tablespoon (15 ml) of neutral oil in a large pan over medium-low heat. Once shimmery, add the garlic and cook, stirring the entire time, until the garlic is lightly golden and fragrant, about 2 minutes. Add the tomato paste and, using a spatula, flatten and break apart until fragrant and vibrant in color, about 2 minutes.

Add the diced tomatoes, crushed tomatoes, 2 teaspoons (10 g) of salt, cumin, black pepper and cayenne (if using). Add 1½ cups (355 ml) of water and turn the heat to high. Once boiling, reduce the heat to low and simmer the sauce until thickened to a consistency similar to a chunky salsa, 10 to 12 minutes.

Add the fried eggplant, potatoes and jalapeños, then stir to mix them in. Cook for 2 minutes, remove the pan from the heat and stir in the vinegar. Serve the mesaka'a warm topped with parsley and with pita bread on the side.

CARAMELIZED ONION HAWAWSHI/ARAYES (PITA POCKET BURGERS)

Egyptian hawawshi—and arayes, *its Levantine sibling—is the closest equivalent to a burger you'll find in the Middle East. And it's just as tasty as one, if not tastier. Hawawshi typically consists of ground beef mixed with onions and spices. It is then stuffed into pita bread and baked or grilled until the meat is cooked through. Vegan "beef" cooks significantly faster than the real deal, and I decided not to mix in raw onion because I didn't think it would cook sufficiently. Instead, I first caramelized the onions to sticky, golden perfection before mixing them with the "meat" which added a whole new and supremely scrumptious flavor to the pockets.*

YIELD: 8 PITA POCKETS

For the Hawawshi

1 tbsp (15 ml) neutral oil

1 large onion, finely chopped

1 serrano pepper, finely chopped (optional)

1 tsp sugar

1½ tsp (6 g) sea salt, divided

2 (12-oz [340-g] each) bricks vegan ground beef

1 tsp garlic powder

1 tsp smoked paprika

1 tsp ground coriander

½ tsp ground nutmeg

½ tsp ground allspice

½ tsp ground cumin

½ tsp ground ginger

¼ tsp ground cardamom

4 medium pita loaves, halved

2 tbsp (30 ml) olive oil

To Serve

Chopped fresh parsley

Garlic tahini sauce

Heat the oil over medium heat in a medium skillet. Once shimmery, add the onion and serrano (if using). Sauté for 2 minutes, stirring occasionally, until the onion is lightly golden at the edges. Add the sugar and ½ teaspoon of salt, stir and turn the heat down to medium. Caramelize the onion, stirring occasionally, until softened and deep golden in color, about 15 minutes. Remove the skillet from the heat and let the onion cool to room temperature.

Preheat the oven to 350°F (180°C).

In a large bowl, combine the caramelized onion, vegan ground beef, garlic powder, smoked paprika, coriander, nutmeg, allspice, cumin, ginger, cardamom and 1 teaspoon of salt. Mix well. Lightly warm the pita pockets to make them easy to open, then stuff them with the meat mixture.

Brush each pocket with olive oil on both sides. Place them on a grilling skillet or a sheet pan and bake them for 7 minutes. Flip the pitas and bake them for 8 minutes, or until the meat is cooked. Serve immediately topped with parsley with a side of garlic tahini.

HARISSA FRIED "CHICKEN" WITH ZA'ATAR FRIES

Thanks to the worldwide presence of major fast-food franchises, fried chicken has become a favorite all across the Middle East. I made classic buttermilk fried "chicken" infused with bold North African flavors for some vegan finger-lickin' goodness. Paired with Levantine-inspired za'atar french fries, this combo is the perfect way to get that Middle Eastern takeout vibe and deliciousness.

YIELD: 4 SERVINGS

For the Fried "Chicken"
2 cubes no-chicken bouillon

2 (16-oz [454-g]) blocks super firm tofu, broken into chunks

1 cup (240 ml) unsweetened plant milk

½ cup (120 ml) vegan cream

2 tbsp (30 ml) apple cider vinegar

1½ cups (190 g) all-purpose flour

3 tbsp (35 g) nutritional yeast

1 tbsp (10 g) harissa seasoning

1 tbsp (10 g) garlic powder

1 tbsp (10 g) onion powder

½ tbsp (8 g) sea salt

1 tsp Aleppo pepper

1 tsp black pepper

1 tsp ground ginger

1 tsp ground coriander

1 tsp dried thyme

1 tsp dried oregano

1½ cups (45 g) vegan cornflakes

½ cup (120 ml) neutral oil

Tahini sauce, to serve

For the Sauce
½ cup (120 g) harissa paste

1 tbsp (15 ml) maple syrup

For the Fries
16 oz (454 g) frozen french fries

1 tbsp (15 ml) neutral oil

2 tbsp (14 g) za'atar

1 tsp sea salt

Whisk together the bouillon and 4 cups (960 ml) of hot water in a large bowl until the bouillon is fully dissolved. Add the tofu, cover and soak for 15 to 20 minutes.

In the meantime, combine the milk, cream, ½ cup (120 ml) of water and the vinegar in a large bowl. Let it curdle for 5 minutes to create "buttermilk."

In a deep plate, add the flour, nutritional yeast, harissa seasoning, garlic powder, onion powder, salt, Aleppo pepper, black pepper, ginger, coriander, thyme and oregano. Mix well to combine.

Taking one piece of tofu at a time, gently squeeze to release the excess broth. Dunk the tofu in the buttermilk mixture, then roll it into the flour mixture until completely coated. Place each piece on a plate and set it aside.

Mix the cornflakes into the remaining flour mixture and stir until well combined. Taking one coated piece at a time, dunk the tofu back into the buttermilk mixture, then roll it into the flour-cornflake mixture until completely coated.

In a large skillet, heat the oil over medium heat. Once lightly smoking, fry the tofu in batches until it is golden and crispy on all sides, 2 to 3 minutes per side. Place the fried tofu on paper towels and set it aside.

Preheat the oven to 420°F (215°C) and line two sheet pans with parchment paper: one for the tofu and the other for the fries.

To make the sauce, whisk together the harissa paste, ½ cup (120 ml) of water and the maple syrup until well incorporated. Taking one piece of tofu at a time, dunk it into the harissa sauce until completely coated. Transfer it to the tofu sheet pan. Bake the tofu for 10 minutes, or until crispy.

Meanwhile, add the french fries and the oil to a large bowl. Toss until the fries are well coated. Transfer to the other sheet pan and bake until golden and crispy, about 25 minutes. Remove the sheet pan from the oven and sprinkle the fries with the za'atar and salt. Toss to coat.

Serve the tofu tenders and fries immediately with the remaining harissa sauce and some tahini on the side.

COMFORTING SOUPS AND COZY STEWS

In the Middle East, soups and stews are a way of life. There's a type for every occasion, from the tomato-based, one-pot wonders to the light, brothy Ramadan soups to the celebratory, intricately spiced stews. There's also one for every palate because the flavor profiles are so varied: from simple and comforting soups, such as Adas bel Hamoud (page 87), to multilayered decadent ones such as Orzo Harira (page 95).

While working on this chapter, I learned a lot about the similarities and differences in the cuisines of the region. For one thing, I got to know more about Iranian cuisine, which led to the development of two of my favorite recipes in this chapter and book: Jackfruit Khoresh-e Fesenjoon (page 84) and Ash Reshteh (page 79). I also discovered a few relatively obscure, but utterly scrumptious recipes, such as the Iraqi Torshana (page 80) and the Palestinian Seitan, Swiss Chard and Chickpea Sumakiyah (page 91). I can't wait for you to try them!

All the recipes here are ones I gravitate toward when I'm missing home and they always leave my heart—and belly—feeling warm and full. I hope they'll leave you feeling immersed in comfort and deliciousness too!

ASH RESHTEH (NOODLES, GREENS AND LEGUMES SOUP)

Though I only discovered ash reshteh *recently, it has quickly climbed its way to the top of my cozy meal list. This protein-packed, herb-loaded sour noodle soup is as comforting as it's bold and bright. The combination of spinach, dill, parsley, cilantro and mint in the soup base—rather than as a topping—was one I hadn't encountered before. I found it immensely enjoyable, and the crispy onion topping adds wonderful umami. Two ingredients distinguish this soup: reshteh, an Iranian thick noodle, and liquid* kashk, *a sour yogurt product. I played with a few variations to find the best vegan substitutions and the end result is magnificent.*

YIELD: 6 SERVINGS

For the Ash Reshteh

2 tbsp (30 ml) neutral oil

1 large onion, chopped

3–4 medium cloves garlic, minced

10 oz (284 g) spinach, chopped

1 large bunch parsley, chopped

1 large bunch cilantro, chopped

1 large bunch dill, chopped

4 scallions, chopped

1 tsp ground turmeric

1 tsp dried mint

1 tsp sea salt

2 no-chicken or vegetable bouillon cubes

1½ cups (246 g) cooked chickpeas

1½ cups (266 g) cooked red kidney beans

1½ cups (297 g) cooked brown lentils

½ cup (120 ml) vegan cooking cream

8 oz (227 g) fettuccine noodles

¼ cup (60 ml) lemon juice

Mint leaves, to serve

For the Onion Topping

1 tbsp (15 ml) neutral oil

1 small onion, thinly sliced

½ tsp sugar (optional)

½ tsp sea salt

For the Ash Reshteh, heat the oil in a Dutch oven or thick bottomed pot over medium heat. Once shimmery, add the onion and cook until completely softened and golden brown, about 15 minutes. Add the garlic, stirring constantly, until fragrant, about 1 minute. Add the spinach, parsley, cilantro, dill, scallions, turmeric, dried mint and salt. Stir for 1 to 2 minutes.

Add the bouillon, chickpeas, red kidney beans and brown lentils along with 4½ cups (1 L) of water. Turn the heat to high. Once boiling, reduce the heat to low and whisk in the cream until dissolved. Simmer for 5 minutes, then add the noodles. Gently stir to prevent the noodles from clumping together. Cover and cook, stirring occasionally, until the stew has thickened and the noodles are soft, but firm (al dente), 15 to 20 minutes. Remove the pot from the heat and stir in the lemon juice.

While the noodles are cooking, make the crispy onion topping. Line a plate with a paper towel. Heat the oil in a medium skillet over medium heat. Once shimmery, add the onion and cook for 5 minutes, stirring occasionally. Add the sugar (if using) and salt. Cook until the onion is golden and caramelized, about 7 minutes. Transfer the onion to the plate.

Serve immediately topped with the caramelized onion and fresh mint.

TORSHANA (DRIED FRUIT-TVP-MUSHROOM STEW)

Torshana, also known as qaysi, *is a sweet and sour Iraqi dish most commonly served during the month of Ramadan because of its high nutritional value. What makes torshana special is the use of dried fruit as the primary ingredient for the stew base. Pairing it with bold spices, such as saffron and cardamom, results in a truly unique dish. I used chunky beef-style TVP as well as mushrooms in this recipe to provide two meaty textures as a contrast to the softness of the stewed fruit. Served topped with toasted nuts and a side of rice, torshana is a great way to add some pizzazz to your weeknight dinner lineup.*

YIELD: 6 TO 8 SERVINGS

For the Torshana

½ cup (100 g) dried apricots

½ cup (100 g) dried figs

¼ cup (50 g) Deglet Nour dates

3 tbsp (45 g) vegan butter

2 medium onions, chopped

1 cup (100 g) cremini mushrooms, sliced

2 cups (320 g) chunky TVP, soaked in water for 30 minutes, rinsed and dried

¼ cup (35 g) raisins

1 tsp ground ginger

½ tsp ground cardamom

Pinch of saffron

1 tsp black pepper

1 tsp sea salt

3 tbsp (50 g) tomato paste

¼ cup (50 g) granulated sugar

To Serve

Slivered almonds, toasted

Chopped scallions

Chopped fresh cilantro

White rice

To make the torshana, place the apricots, figs and dates in separate bowls and cover the fruit with warm water. Soak the fruit for 30 minutes, then drain and gently squeeze the fruit. Roughly chop the fruit and set it aside.

Melt the vegan butter in a Dutch oven or heavy bottomed pot over medium heat. Once bubbling, add the onions and mushrooms. Cook for 5 minutes, stirring occasionally, or until the onions are lightly golden at the edges. Add the reconstituted TVP and cook, stirring intermittently, until the TVP is crispy, 10 to 12 minutes.

Add the apricots, figs, dates and raisins and cook for 2 to 3 minutes, stirring now and then, until lightly toasted. Add the ginger, cardamom, saffron, black pepper and salt. Stir together for 30 seconds, then add the tomato paste. Stir the tomato paste until all the ingredients are coated, about 2 minutes.

Add the sugar and 1 quart (960 ml) of water. Turn the heat to high, bring the stew to a boil then lower to a simmer. Cook it until the TVP chunks and dried fruit are tender and juicy, 20 to 25 minutes.

Serve hot topped with almonds, scallions and cilantro, with a side of white rice.

ROASTED CAULIFLOWER, TEMPEH AND CHICKPEA MOGHRABIEH (BROTHY SPICED PEARL COUSCOUS)

Moghrabieh *is a beautifully hearty Lebanese soup. The dish has two main components: a gorgeous broth highlighting Lebanese 7 spice and caraway seed, and perfectly chewy moghrabieh, which is almost identical to pearl couscous. While the soup typically features chicken, I used roasted tempeh and cauliflower to provide amazing texture and flavor. This is the perfect soup to sip on a cold day, and it's a great winter dinner to share with loved ones.*

YIELD: 6 SERVINGS

For the Soup

2 (16-oz [454-g]) blocks tempeh, chopped

1 small head cauliflower, broken into florets

1½ cups (246 g) cooked chickpeas

2 tsp (8 g) Lebanese 7 Spice (page 45), divided

2 tsp (10 g) sea salt, divided

1 tbsp (15 ml) neutral oil

1 tbsp (15 g) vegan butter

1 large onion, chopped

6 medium sage leaves, thinly sliced

1 tsp ground caraway

1 tsp black pepper

1 cube vegetable bouillon

For the Moghrabieh

1 tbsp (15 g) vegan butter

1½ cups (336 g) moghrabieh or pearl couscous

½ tsp dried thyme

½ tsp ground nutmeg

½ tsp ground cinnamon

1 tsp sea salt

To Serve

Chopped fresh parsley

Chopped scallions

Lemon slices

Sautéed honeynut squash and bell peppers

Preheat the oven to 420°F (215°C).

In a large bowl, mix together the tempeh, cauliflower, chickpeas, 1 teaspoon of Lebanese 7 spice, 1 teaspoon of salt and the oil until well incorporated. Transfer the mixture to a sheet pan and roast, flipping once or twice to cook evenly, until everything is crispy, about 30 minutes. Remove the sheet pan from the oven and set it aside.

In a large pot, melt the vegan butter over medium heat. Once bubbling, add the onion and cook until softened and golden, about 10 minutes. Add the sage and cook, stirring occasionally, until fragrant, about 2 minutes. Add the remaining Lebanese 7 spice and salt along with the caraway and black pepper. Stir together for 30 seconds. Add the bouillon, 5 cups (1.2 L) of water and the roasted cauliflower, chickpeas and tempeh. Turn the heat to high. Once boiling, reduce the heat and simmer for 5 minutes. Remove the pot from the heat.

To make the moghrabieh, bring 2¼ cups (540 ml) of water to a boil in a medium pot. Stir in the butter, moghrabieh, thyme, nutmeg, cinnamon and salt. Reduce the heat to low, cover and simmer for 10 minutes, or until almost all the water has been absorbed. Remove the pot from the heat and let it sit covered for 5 minutes. Fluff the moghrabieh and set it aside.

Plate the moghrabieh, then ladle the broth over it. Top with more moghrabieh and garnish with parsley, scallions and lemon. Serve with your choice of side dish, if desired.

JACKFRUIT KHORESH-E FESENJOON (POMEGRANATE WALNUT STEW)

Khoresh-e Fesenjoon was love at first bite for me. This Iranian stew—which features toasted walnuts, pomegranate molasses and a lovely mix of warm spices—will similarly sweep your taste buds away with its boldly earthy, sweet and sour flavors. I swapped the traditional chicken with jackfruit, and I kept the jackfruit in unbroken chunks that I seared to golden perfection before cooking them in the sauce. The result was a spectacularly savory stew I'd happily eat and serve on any given day.

YIELD: 4 SERVINGS

For the Stew

8 oz (227 g) walnuts

1 cube vegetable bouillon

3 tbsp (45 ml) neutral oil, divided

2 (40-oz [1.13-kg]) cans young jackfruit, drained

1 large onion, chopped

4 medium cloves garlic, minced

Peel of ½ navel orange

1 cinnamon stick

½ tsp ground turmeric

½ tsp ground nutmeg

½ tsp ground coriander

½ tsp cayenne (optional)

¼ tsp saffron

1 tsp sea salt

½ cup (169 g) pomegranate molasses

2 tbsp (30 ml) maple syrup

2 tbsp (30 ml) soy sauce

1½ cups (246 g) cooked chickpeas

To Serve

Pomegranate arils

Chopped fresh parsley

Vermicelli rice

To make the stew, heat a large skillet over high heat. Once lightly smoking, add the walnuts, making sure to distribute them evenly. Toast the walnuts, stirring occasionally, until fragrant and lightly golden, 4 to 5 minutes. Watch closely to avoid burning. Transfer them to a plate and set them aside to cool.

Once the walnuts are at room temperature, transfer them to a food processor and pulse until the walnuts are broken down. Add the vegetable bouillon and 2 cups (480 ml) of water. Pulse it until completely smooth and creamy. Set the mixture aside.

In a large pan or skillet, heat 2 tablespoons (30 ml) of neutral oil over medium heat. Once shimmery, add the jackfruit chunks in batches and sear until golden on all sides, about 2 minutes per side. Transfer the jackfruit to a plate and set it aside.

Add the remaining 1 tablespoon (15 ml) of neutral oil to the same pan used for the jackfruit. Once shimmery, add the onion and sauté, stirring occasionally, until soft and golden, about 10 minutes. Add the garlic and cook for 2 minutes, or until the garlic is golden.

Add the orange peel, cinnamon stick, turmeric, nutmeg, coriander, cayenne (if using), saffron and salt. Cook for 30 seconds, stirring to distribute evenly, then add the pomegranate molasses, maple syrup, soy sauce, walnut mixture, seared jackfruit and chickpeas. Mix well, cover and turn the heat to high.

Once the stew is boiling, lower the heat to medium-low and crack the lid so the stew is only partially covered. Let the stew reduce until the sauce has thickened to a consistency similar to that of a curry. Remove the pot from the heat.

Serve immediately topped with pomegranate arils and parsley with a side of vermicelli rice.

ADAS BEL HAMOUD (SOUR LENTIL SOUP)

Adas bel hamoud, *or sour lentils, is a hearty yet simple soup. It's a great weeknight option, especially during colder months. This soup originates from Lebanon and typically combines brown lentils with Swiss chard and lemon juice. I've opted for mustard greens instead to add a peppery kick and also added potatoes and celery for both texture and a creamier, more herbaceous flavor.*

YIELD: 5 TO 6 SERVINGS

For the Soup

3 tbsp (45 ml) olive oil

3 medium onions, chopped

4 medium Yukon gold potatoes, cubed

3 ribs celery, chopped

2 large cloves garlic, minced

2 cups (32 g) finely chopped cilantro

1 tsp sumac

1 tsp Lebanese 7 spice (page 45)

1 tsp black pepper

2 cubes vegetable bouillon

1 large bunch mustard greens, Swiss chard, collards or turnip greens, leaves and stems, roughly chopped

3 cups (594 g) cooked lentils

⅓ cup (80 ml) lemon juice

To Serve

Aleppo pepper

Lemon wedges

To make the soup, heat the olive oil in a Dutch oven or heavy bottomed pot over medium heat. Once shimmery, add the onions and cook until translucent and golden at the edges, about 5 minutes. Add the potatoes, stir well and cook for 5 minutes. Add the celery and garlic. Cook, stirring constantly to prevent burning, until the garlic is fragrant, about 1 minute.

Reduce the heat to medium-low, add the cilantro and stir until just wilted, about 1 minute. Add the sumac, Lebanese 7 spice and black pepper. Stir together for 30 seconds. Add the vegetable bouillon along with 5 cups (1.2 L) of water and turn the heat to high. Once boiling, reduce the heat to low and add the greens. Cover and simmer until the potatoes are tender, about 15 minutes.

Add the lentils and continue cooking just until the lentils are warmed, 2 to 3 minutes. Remove the pot from the heat and stir in the lemon juice. Serve the soup hot, sprinkled with Aleppo pepper with a couple of lemon wedges on the side.

SHORBET KHODAR (VEGETABLE SOUP) WITH PULLED TRUMPET MUSHROOM "CHICKEN"

Almost every culture in the world has its own take on vegetable soup. This is a vegan version of the Egyptian one. While there's nothing revolutionary about this soup, its beauty lies in its gorgeous simplicity. The most distinctive aspect of Egyptian shorbet khodar *is its heavy use of celery, which lends it a lovely herbaceousness. I added my spin to this recipe by using freshly ground toasted spices and red kidney beans. For the traditional chicken breasts, I substituted poultry-seasoned, shredded trumpet mushrooms, crisped to perfection and packed with umami. This is my number one go-to soup on rainy days, and it is the definition of a culinary hug.*

YIELD: 5 TO 6 SERVINGS

For the Soup

1 tsp cumin seeds (optional)

1 tsp coriander seeds (optional)

1 tbsp (15 ml) plus 1 tsp neutral oil, divided

1 large onion, diced

1 lb (454 g) Yukon Gold potatoes, peeled and cubed

1 cup (110 g) chopped green beans

2 medium carrots, peeled and chopped

6 ribs celery, chopped

3 medium cloves garlic, minced

2 tbsp (22 g) poultry seasoning, such as McKay's Chicken Style Seasoning®

1 tsp sea salt

1 tsp white pepper

1 cup (134 g) frozen green peas

1½ cups (266 g) cooked red kidney beans

For the Mushrooms

6 large trumpet mushrooms

1 tbsp (15 ml) neutral oil

1 tbsp (14 g) poultry seasoning

To Serve

Lime wedges

To make the soup, if using cumin and coriander seeds, heat 1 teaspoon of oil in a Dutch oven over medium-low heat. Once shimmery, add the seeds and toast them until crackling and fragrant, 30 to 60 seconds. Remove the seeds from the pot and grind them in a mortar and or small food processor. Set them aside.

Add 1 tablespoon (15 ml) of oil to the pot over medium heat. Once shimmery, add the onion and cook until slightly softened, about 2 minutes. Add the potatoes and green beans and cook until golden at the edges, about 10 minutes. Add the carrots, celery and garlic and cook until the garlic is fragrant, 4 to 5 minutes. Add the toasted cumin and coriander (if using) along with the poultry seasoning, salt and white pepper. Stir together for 30 seconds to combine.

Add 5 cups (1.2 L) of water and the green peas, then turn the heat to high. Once the soup is boiling, lower the heat to simmer, cover and cook until the potatoes and green beans are fork tender, 10 to 15 minutes. Add the kidney beans, cook for 1 to 2 minutes to warm then remove the soup from the heat.

To prepare the mushrooms, use a fork and, starting at the bottom of the mushroom, firmly drag the fork down toward the cap to shred. Reserve the caps for another recipe. The mushroom shreds should resemble pulled string cheese. Once done, heat the oil in a large nonstick skillet. Once shimmery, add the pulled mushrooms. Cook for 2 minutes, or until the mushrooms release water and soften. Stir in the poultry seasoning. Cook the mushrooms, stirring occasionally, until no moisture remains and the mushrooms are golden and crispy, 10 to 12 minutes. Remove the skillet from the heat.

Serve the soup warm, topped generously with the crispy pulled mushrooms and with lime wedges on the side.

SEITAN, SWISS CHARD AND CHICKPEA SUMAKIYAH (SUMAC TAHINI STEW)

Sumakiyah, *which gets its name from sumac, is an ancient Palestinian stew that's tangy, rich and creamy. I first stumbled upon this dish in cookbook author May S. Bsisu's* The Arab Table, *and as soon as I noticed the recipe heavily featured both sumac and tahini, I was sold! Veganizing sumakiyah was tricky because lamb meat is the star of the original, but after exploring a few options, I finally settled on using homemade seitan "steaks." This stew is one of a kind, and I can't recommend it enough.*

YIELD: 5 TO 6 SERVINGS

For the Stew

1 cup (96 g) sumac

3 tbsp (24 g) all-purpose flour

3 tbsp (45 ml) neutral oil, divided

3 medium Succulent "Steaks" (page 27), cubed

2 medium yellow onions, chopped

4 medium cloves garlic, peeled

1 serrano or habanero pepper (optional)

1 tbsp (8 g) dill seeds

1 tsp nutmeg

1 tsp white pepper

1 tsp sea salt

½ tsp ground cardamom

2 cups (328 g) cooked chickpeas

1 bay leaf

2 bunches Swiss chard, chopped

½ cup (125 g) tahini

¼ cup (60 ml) lemon juice

To Serve

Pomegranate arils

Chopped fresh parsley

Flatbread

To make the stew, whisk together the sumac and 2 cups (480 ml) of water in a large saucepan. Boil the mixture over high heat for 7 minutes, whisking occasionally, then remove it from the heat. Process the mixture using an immersion blender, then strain it through a fine-mesh sieve into a large bowl. Discard the pulp in the sieve.

In a small bowl, whisk together the flour with ½ cup (120 ml) of water until fully dissolved. Add the flour slurry to the strained sumac mixture and stir it to combine. Set it aside.

Heat 2 tablespoons (30 ml) of oil in a Dutch oven or pot over medium heat. Once lightly smoking, add the cubed steak and cook, stirring occasionally, until golden and crispy. Transfer the steak to a plate and set it aside.

Heat the remaining 1 tablespoon (15 ml) of oil over medium heat. Once shimmery, add the onions and cook until golden, about 10 minutes.

Place the garlic, serrano (if using) and dill seeds in a mortar or food processor. Grind/pulse it until broken down but not completely pulverized. Add the mixture to the pot, stir and cook for 2 minutes, or until fragrant.

Add the nutmeg, white pepper, salt, cardamom and chickpeas. Cook for 1 minute, stirring to distribute the spices, then add 3 cups (720 ml) of water, the bay leaf, seitan and Swiss chard. Turn the heat to high, bring it to a boil then lower the heat to a simmer. Cook, uncovered, for 5 minutes before stirring in the sumac mixture.

Cook uncovered until the stew has thickened to a gravy-like consistency, about 15 minutes. Stir in the tahini and mix well. Cook for 2 to 3 minutes, or until desired thickness is reached. The consistency should be a little thicker than gravy, but still a little runny. Remove the pot from the heat, discard the bay leaf, add the lemon juice and stir.

Serve warm topped with pomegranate arils and parsley, with a side of flatbread.

SHORBET TAMATEM BEL ROZ (ROASTED TOMATO-RICE SOUP)

This recipe takes Jordanian shorbet tamatem bel roz *and gives it a glow up. To create the base, I roasted tomatoes rather than using canned diced ones, and I added a generous helping of roasted garlic along with roasted red bell peppers and sun-dried tomatoes to create layers of flavor. Rather than simply sauté the onions, I caramelized them and mixed in lots of herbs before finishing off with fluffy basmati rice for a truly robust and satisfying soup.*

YIELD: 4 SERVINGS

For the Soup

3 lb (1.4 kg) plum tomatoes, halved

1 large red bell pepper, seeded and halved

8 medium cloves garlic, peeled

3 tbsp (45 ml) olive oil, plus more for topping

1 tsp celery salt or sea salt (optional)

⅓ cup (60 g) jarred sun-dried tomatoes

3 tbsp (48 g) tomato paste

1 tsp Lebanese 7 Spice (page 45)

1 tsp dried thyme

1 tsp dried sage

1 tsp dried marjoram

1 tsp black pepper

1 tsp sea salt

1 tbsp (15 ml) neutral oil

2 medium onions, finely chopped

1 tbsp (15 g) sugar

2 cups (380 g) cooked basmati rice

To Serve

Chopped fresh parsley

Aleppo pepper

Vegan sour cream

Lemon wedges

Preheat the oven to 450°F (232°C) and line a large sheet pan with parchment paper.

Place the tomatoes, bell pepper and garlic on the sheet pan, drizzle with the olive oil, sprinkle with celery salt (if using) and roast undisturbed until lightly charred and juicy, about 40 minutes. Remove the sheet pan from the oven and let the vegetables cool enough to handle, 15 to 20 minutes.

Peel the skin off the roasted red bell peppers. Transfer all the roasted vegetables to a blender along with the sun-dried tomatoes, tomato paste, 7 spice, thyme, sage, marjoram, black pepper and salt. Pulse it until completely broken down and creamy. Set it aside.

Heat the neutral oil in a large pot over medium-low heat. Once shimmery, add the onions and sugar. Cook until the onions are tender and caramelized, about 17 minutes. Add the pureed roasted vegetables and 3½ cups (840 ml) of water. Turn the heat to high and bring it to a boil, then reduce the heat to low. Simmer for 5 minutes, or until the desired thickness is reached. Remove the pot from the heat and stir in the rice.

Serve immediately topped with parsley, Aleppo pepper and vegan sour cream with a couple of lemon wedges on the side. Refrigerate leftovers for up to 5 days.

ORZO HARIRA (LEGUME AND SOURDOUGH SOUP)

Harira, which means "silky," is a type of noodle legume soup that's part of both Algerian and Moroccan cuisines. While the more current versions of harira use a flour slurry, I took the traditional route, which uses sourdough starter to thicken and flavor the soup. I substituted the typically used vermicelli with orzo because I've found that this soup really benefits from a chewier, more substantial pasta variety. This is a hearty, multilayered dish with bright pops of herb, tomato, saffron and fermented flavors perfect for chilly weather.

YIELD: 6 SERVINGS

For the Soup

¼ cup (69 g) active bubbly sourdough starter (see Note)

1 tbsp (8 g) all-purpose flour

2 tbsp (30 ml) olive oil

1 tbsp (15 g) vegan butter

1 large onion, chopped

4–5 medium Campari or 3 medium Roma tomatoes, diced

½ cup (30 g) chopped celery leaves (no ribs)

½ cup (30 g) chopped fresh parsley

½ cup (8 g) chopped fresh cilantro

1 tsp ground cinnamon

1 tsp ground ginger

1 tsp ground turmeric

1 tsp black pepper

1 tsp sea salt

½ tsp saffron, crumbled

2 tbsp (32 g) tomato paste

1 cup (244 g) crushed tomatoes

1 cup (170 g) orzo pasta

1½ cups (246 g) cooked chickpeas

1½ cups (297 g) cooked lentils

To Serve

Parsley

Lemon wedges

In a medium bowl, combine the sourdough starter and flour with ¾ cup (180 ml) of cold or room temperature water. Whisk together until completely smooth; strain the mixture if necessary to ensure there are no lumps. Set it aside.

Heat the olive oil and vegan butter in a Dutch oven or thick bottomed pot over medium heat. Once bubbling, add the onion and cook until softened and golden, about 12 minutes. Add the diced tomatoes and continue cooking until the tomatoes break down and release their juice, about 5 minutes. Add the celery leaves, parsley and cilantro. Mix well and cook until lightly wilted, 1 to 2 minutes. Stir in the cinnamon, ginger, turmeric, black pepper, salt and saffron for about 30 seconds, or until well distributed.

Add the tomato paste and mix it in until all the ingredients are coated, 1 to 2 minutes. Add the crushed tomatoes along with 4 cups (960 ml) of water. Turn the heat to high to bring it to a boil, then reduce the heat to low. Add the orzo, chickpeas and lentils and simmer, stirring frequently to prevent the orzo from sticking or clumping. Cook until the orzo is al dente or slightly under, 15 to 20 minutes.

Add one-third of the sourdough mix while stirring vigorously to prevent lumps from forming. Once well incorporated, add another one-third of the mixture and continue stirring until well incorporated. Add the last of the mixture and repeat. Simmer the harira until it thickens to a consistency similar to chunky chili, or until desired thickness, about 10 minutes. Remove it from the heat.

Serve the harira immediately topped with the parsley with a couple of lemon wedges on the side.

NOTE: Harira is typically made with *khameera baladi*, which is very similar to sourdough and gives traditional harira a unique lightly fermented flavor. If you don't have sourdough starter on hand or would rather omit it, make the following substitution: Instead of 1 tablespoon (8 g) of all-purpose flour, use ⅓ cup (41 g) of all-purpose flour. Mix it with 1 cup (240 ml) of water until completely smooth and follow the same instructions as for the sourdough mixture for when and how to add it.

SUMPTUOUS SALADS

If you've been following my Instagram account, leeksnbeets, for a while, then you know just how much I love salads. Salads seem to get a bad rep because of the sad, boring, wilty-lettuce-and-watery-tomato versions that are served by way too many restaurants and households. Luckily, Middle Eastern culture is both home to and incredibly well suited for great salads, which made crafting the recipes for this chapter a blast!

While a few of the salads here, such as Tabbouleh (page 99) and Fattoush (page 103), are traditional recipes that I adapted for this book, the majority are ones I created myself using Middle Eastern ingredients and flavor profiles. For example, in the "Halloumi" Cheese and Beet Salad with Lemon-Thyme Vinaigrette (page 111) I made a vegan version of halloumi (a traditional Levantine cheese) and paired it with beets and lemons, both of which are common in most Middle Eastern countries.

The Maftoul and Broad Bean Salad with Rosemary-Molasses Vinaigrette (page 100) and Freekeh–Medjool Date Salad with Preserved Lemon Dressing (page 115) both utilize grains that originated in North Africa and the Levant along with other widely used Middle Eastern ingredients such as preserved lemons and broad beans. Then there are recipes such as the Roasted Potato Salad with Sahawiq (page 112), where I combined a culturally neutral ingredient (potatoes) with *sahawiq*, a popular and delectable Yemeni sauce.

Every single salad here was a huge hit in my household, and I'm beyond excited for you to try them.

KALE TABBOULEH (HERBACEOUS BULGUR WHEAT SALAD)

Tabbouleh is one of the most widely recognized Middle Eastern salads for good reason. Originating from the Levant, specifically from Lebanon and Syria, it's as light as it is filling thanks to the combination of hearty bulgur wheat with heaps of fresh parsley, crisp raw veggies and lemon juice. While I love classic tabbouleh, I ramped up the vibrance with the addition of massaged kale. It also provides an extra texture that I find elevates the rest of the salad's components.

YIELD: 2 TO 3 SERVINGS

⅔ cup (95 g) coarse bulgur

2 cups (140 g) kale, packed and chopped, stems removed

¼ cup (60 ml) plus 1 tsp extra virgin olive oil, divided

1 cup (160 g) Persian cucumber, chopped

2 cups (120 g) packed parsley, minced

½ cup (80 g) chopped red onion

1 cup (149 g) cherry tomatoes, quartered

2 tbsp (30 ml) lemon juice

2 tbsp (10 g) dried mint

1 tsp garlic powder

1 tsp sea salt

In a medium pot, bring 1½ cups (360 ml) of water to a boil. Add the bulgur, stir, then lower the heat to a simmer. Cook the bulgur covered for 7 minutes. Remove the pot from the heat and let it sit covered for 10 minutes. Fluff the bulgur with a fork and let it cool to room temperature.

Meanwhile, place the kale in a large bowl. Add 1 teaspoon of extra virgin olive oil. Using your hands, massage the kale for 2 minutes, or until it is soft and tender.

Add the bulgur, cucumbers, parsley, onion, tomatoes, remaining ¼ cup (60 ml) of olive oil, lemon juice, mint, garlic powder and salt to the kale. Using a large spoon, mix it well. Transfer the tabbouleh to a container with an airtight lid and chill it for at least 1 hour before serving.

MAFTOUL (BULGUR WHEAT COUSCOUS) AND BROAD BEAN SALAD WITH ROSEMARY-MOLASSES VINAIGRETTE

Maftoul *translates to "rolled," and it refers to the way this Palestinian tiny pasta is made. Structurally it's similar to pearl couscous, but it has a deeper earthier flavor and more of a bite because it's made from bulgur wheat. While maftoul is traditionally prepared in a brothy stew, this version is a lighter, brighter preparation that better allows its gorgeous flavor to shine. I paired it with vibrant broad beans, mild and creamy delicata squash and umami-loaded sun-dried tomato. The dish is rounded out with a rosemary-molasses vinaigrette that has sweet, herbaceous and slightly bitter notes. This salad is a spectacular dinner option, especially when transitioning from late summer to early fall.*

YIELD: 4 SERVINGS

For the Salad

1 cup (155 g) dry maftoul, pearl couscous or fregula pasta, cooked according to package instructions

1½ cups (180 g) shelled broad (fava) beans

1 cup (175 g) delicata squash, seeded, chopped and sauteed

1 bunch parsley, chopped

½ cup (90 g) jarred sun-dried tomatoes, chopped, plus 1 tbsp (15 ml) oil from the jar

½ cup (80 g) thinly sliced Persian cucumber

¼ cup (28 g) thinly sliced radish

¼ cup (25 g) shelled pistachios, roughly chopped

1 tbsp (10 g) hemp hearts (optional)

1 tsp sea salt

For the Dressing

⅓ cup (80 ml) extra virgin olive oil

¼ cup (60 ml) date vinegar (or malt or balsamic vinegar)

2 tbsp (40 g) molasses

2 tbsp (3 g) fresh rosemary leaves

1 tsp garlic powder

1 tsp sea salt

½ tsp black pepper

To make the salad, add the maftoul, broad beans, squash, parsley, sun-dried tomatoes and 1 tablespoon (15 ml) of their oil, cucumber, radishes, pistachios, hemp hearts (if using) and salt to a large bowl. Toss until well combined.

To make the dressing, add the oil, vinegar, molasses, rosemary, garlic powder, salt and black pepper to a blender. Pulse it until completely smooth and well incorporated.

Right before serving, pour half the dressing into the salad and toss. Reserve the other half to serve on the side. Serve the salad chilled or at room temperature.

FATTOUSH (VEGGIE SUMAC SALAD WITH FRIED PITA "CROUTONS")

Fattoush is proof that sumac and pita bread make anything better. At its core, this Levantine dish is a simple chunky salad. It's the tangy dressing and the pita "croutons" that make it one of the most loved and well-known Middle Eastern recipes. While the pita bread here is usually fried, you could toast it in the oven without any oil, if you prefer.

YIELD: 3 TO 4 SERVINGS

For the Pita "Croutons"

¼ cup (60 ml) neutral oil

3 medium loaves The Best Pita Bread (page 19), cut into squares

For the Dressing

¼ cup (60 ml) extra virgin olive oil

2 tbsp (30 ml) lemon juice

1 tbsp (20 g) pomegranate molasses

1 medium clove garlic, finely minced

½ tsp Aleppo pepper

1 tsp sea salt

For the Salad

2 heads romaine lettuce, chopped

1 pint (298 g) snacking rainbow tomatoes, halved

1 English cucumber, thinly sliced

6–7 medium radishes, thinly sliced

2 shallots, thinly sliced

¼ cup (25 g) fresh mint leaves

2 tbsp (7 g) dill fronds

2 tsp (5 g) sumac, plus more for topping

To make the pita croutons, line a plate with a paper towel. Heat the neutral oil in a medium-sized pan over medium heat. Once shimmery, add the pita squares in batches and fry them until golden and crispy on both sides, about 1 minute per side. Watch the pita closely because it can overcook very quickly. Transfer them to the plate and set it aside.

To make the dressing, add the extra virgin olive oil, lemon juice, pomegranate molasses, garlic, Aleppo pepper and salt to a jar with an airtight lid. Seal the jar and shake it until the ingredients are well incorporated.

To serve, place the lettuce, tomatoes, cucumber, radishes, shallots, mint, dill and sumac in a large bowl. Add half the dressing and mix together well. Top the salad with the pita croutons and more sumac. Serve it with the remaining dressing on the side.

ARTICHOKE "BASTERMA" ("BEEF PROSCIUTTO") SALAD WITH TAMARIND-POMEGRANATE DRESSING

Basterma is a delightfully salty cured meat that's widely used in Egypt, and it's usually cooked with eggs. I like to think of it as Middle Eastern halal prosciutto. This was one of the trickier animal products to veganize because reproducing the texture was difficult, but it's so unique and delicious that I had to keep trying. Luckily, I was able to recreate it using marinated vegan jerky, and the result is truly delectable. I paired it with other little-known and/or underrated Middle Eastern ingredients such as artichokes, tamarind and pomegranate for a distinctive, yummy salad.

YIELD: 2 SERVINGS

For the Dressing

1 tbsp (15 g) seedless tamarind paste

1 tbsp (20 g) pomegranate molasses

¼ cup (60 ml) olive oil

3 tbsp (45 ml) maple syrup

1 tbsp (15 ml) artichoke marinade

1 tsp garlic powder

1 tsp sea salt

1 tsp black pepper

For the Salad

1 tbsp (15 ml) soy sauce

1 tsp neutral oil

1 tsp beet powder

3 oz (85 g) vegan jerky

4 cups (170 g) spring mix or baby spinach

4 oz (112 g) grilled quartered artichoke hearts (from a jar, removed from the marinade)

1 medium shallot, sliced

½ medium zucchini, shaved into strips then rolled

¼ cup (43 g) pomegranate arils

2 tbsp (7 g) dill fronds

1 tsp Aleppo pepper

Sea salt

To make the dressing, add the tamarind paste, pomegranate molasses, olive oil, maple syrup, artichoke marinade, garlic powder, salt and black pepper to a blender. Pulse it until completely smooth.

To make the salad, whisk together the soy sauce, neutral oil and beet powder. Add the vegan jerky. Let it sit for 15 minutes to tenderize, then discard the marinade or use it in another recipe.

To plate the salad, start with a base of spring mix. Top it with the artichoke hearts, shallot, zucchini, pomegranate arils, dill, Aleppo pepper and salt. Drizzle the salad with a little dressing. Serve it immediately with more dressing on the side.

DOLMA (HERBY TVP AND GRAPEVINE) SALAD

When you're craving stuffed grapevine leaves, but you don't want to go through the lengthy process of making them, this salad is the answer. Inspired by the cold appetizer version of dolma, this salad combines chopped grapevine leaves and brine with grains, chicken-style TVP (textured vegetable protein), tomatoes, herbs, walnuts and raisins. It makes a delicious and nutritious meal. I used einkorn, a hearty ancient grain that can be substituted with barley or wheat berries, to add a pleasantly substantial chewy texture. I also kept the dressing light to allow the freshness and herbaceous saltiness of the grapevine leaves to shine. This salad has become a staple in my kitchen thanks to its uniquely Middle Eastern flavor profile and irresistible savoriness.

YIELD: 3 TO 4 SERVINGS

1½ cups (240 g) cooked einkorn or grain of choice

1 tsp ground coriander

1 tsp poultry seasoning

1 tbsp (15 ml) neutral oil

1 medium onion, chopped

¾ cup (120 g) TVP, soaked in water for 30 minutes, then rinsed and dried (or substitute veggie crumbles or lentils)

1 tsp Aleppo pepper

½ tsp ground cinnamon

½ tsp ground cumin

1 tsp sea salt

10–12 grapevine leaves, chopped plus 1 tbsp (15 ml) brine from the jar

½ cup (90 g) chopped tomatoes

½ cup (30 g) chopped fresh dill

⅓ cup (25 g) chopped fresh parsley

¼ cup (4 g) chopped fresh cilantro

¼ cup (40 g) golden raisins

¼ cup (30 g) chopped toasted walnuts

3 tbsp (45 ml) extra virgin olive oil

¼ cup (60 ml) lemon juice

In a large bowl, combine the einkorn, coriander and poultry seasoning. Set it aside for 15 minutes to allow the flavors to be absorbed.

Heat the neutral oil in a large skillet over medium heat. Once shimmering, add the onion and cook for 10 minutes, or until softened and golden. Add the TVP, Aleppo pepper, cinnamon, cumin and salt.

Cook, stirring occasionally, until the TVP is crispy, about 7 minutes. Remove the skillet from the heat.

Combine the cooked TVP, grapevine leaves, tomatoes, dill, parsley, cilantro, raisins, walnuts, olive oil and lemon juice with the einkorn and mix well. Serve at room temperature or chilled.

GRILLED CORN AND LENTIL SALAD WITH SUMAC AND ALEPPO PEPPER VINAIGRETTE

During summertime in Egypt, freshly roasted corn is a beloved snack you can usually purchase straight from the farmers' wagons. This salad, a favorite in my household, highlights the succulence of roasted corn by combining it with simple fresh vegetables and brown lentils. The vinaigrette—inspired by Levantine cuisine—packs a ton of zest and a hint of spice. It perfectly balances the sweetness of the roasted corn and the mildness of the rest of the ingredients.

YIELD: 3 TO 4 SERVINGS

For the Salad
Kernels from 2 large ears of corn

1 tsp smoked paprika

½ tsp black pepper

4 cups (268 g) chopped kale, stems removed

1 tsp extra virgin olive oil

1½ cups (297 g) cooked brown lentils

1½ cups (224 g) sliced cherry tomatoes

1 large shallot, chopped

3 medium radishes, sliced

1 jalapeño, seeded and chopped

3 tbsp (17 g) chopped fresh mint

¼ cup (34 g) pine nuts, toasted

Pomegranate arils, to serve

For the Vinaigrette
¼ cup (60 ml) olive oil

2 tbsp (30 ml) lemon juice

1½ tbsp (30 g) pomegranate molasses

1 medium clove garlic, minced

1 tbsp (15 ml) maple syrup

½ tbsp (5 g) nigella seeds (optional)

1 tsp sumac

1 tsp za'atar

1 tsp Aleppo pepper

1 tsp sea salt

Heat a large cast-iron skillet over high heat until lightly smoky. Add the corn kernels and cook, stirring occasionally, until lightly charred. Remove the skillet from the heat. Stir in the smoked paprika and black pepper, then let it cool to room temperature.

To make the vinaigrette, whisk together the olive oil, lemon juice, pomegranate molasses, garlic, maple syrup, nigella seeds (if using), sumac, za'atar, Aleppo pepper and salt.

In a large bowl, combine the kale with the olive oil and massage until the kale is tender and vibrant green, about 3 minutes. Add the lentils, tomatoes, shallot, radishes, jalapeño and mint. Toss with half of the vinaigrette.

Serve chilled or at room temperature topped with the pine nuts and pomegranate arils with the remaining vinaigrette on the side.

"HALLOUMI" CHEESE AND BEET SALAD WITH LEMON-THYME VINAIGRETTE

Halloumi is a type of cheese commonly used in Levantine cuisine. It is similar in texture to firm mozzarella and paneer. While there are many vegan versions of Halloumi out there, most of them use tofu which may look like Halloumi, but doesn't taste like it. My sister-in-law first shared this cashew-based version with me two years ago, and I've adjusted the method quite a bit over time. The result is an outrageously tasty vegan fried Halloumi that's astoundingly reminiscent of the real thing. It's salty and crispy with a melt-in-your-mouth texture that pairs gorgeously with the sweetness and earthiness of the steamed beets. It makes this salad an absolute delight.

YIELD: 2 SERVINGS

For the Halloumi Cheese

2 cups (280 g) cashews, soaked in boiling water for 20 minutes

½ cup (65 g) tapioca starch

¼ cup (55 g) refined coconut oil

2 tbsp (10 g) agar agar

2 tsp (10 g) sea salt

1 tsp lemon juice

¼ cup (60 ml) neutral oil to cook

For the Vinaigrette

¼ cup (60 ml) extra virgin olive oil

2 tbsp (30 ml) lemon juice

1 tbsp (2 g) fresh lemon thyme or thyme leaves

1 tsp lemon zest

1 tsp black pepper

1 tsp sea salt

For the Salad

4 cups (170 g) spring mix

1 large yellow beet, steamed and cubed

1 large red beet, steamed and cubed

1 large shallot, sliced

1 cup (149 g) cherry tomatoes, halved

1 tbsp (10 g) hemp hearts

To make the cheese, line a square 9-inch (22-cm) pan with parchment paper and set it aside.

Drain the cashews and transfer them to a food processor along with the tapioca starch, coconut oil, agar agar, salt, lemon juice and 2 cups (480 ml) of cold water. Pulse it until completely smooth and creamy, then transfer the mixture to a medium saucepan.

Cook the mixture over medium heat, whisking the entire time to avoid it from getting lumpy. Make sure to use a sturdy whisk because the mixture will get very thick.

Once bubbling, lower the heat to medium-low and continue whisking until the mixture resembles bread dough and is pulling from the sides, about 2 minutes. Remove the pan from the heat and immediately transfer the mixture to the square pan and evenly flatten using a spatula. The mixture will set very quickly.

Place the pan in the freezer to set for 1 hour, then refrigerate until ready to use. The Halloumi cheese will keep for up to 5 days in the fridge or up to 1 month in the freezer. Just thaw it overnight in the fridge before using. The Halloumi is best served fresh so make sure your salad is fully assembled prior to frying the cheese.

Once ready to cook, line a plate with a paper towel. Chop the Halloumi cheese into strips resembling mozzarella sticks. Heat the neutral oil over medium in a grilling or regular skillet. Once shimmery, add the cheese strips and fry them until golden and crispy on all sides, about 1 minute per side. Transfer them to the lined plate.

To make the vinaigrette, combine the olive oil, lemon juice, lemon thyme, lemon zest, black pepper and salt in a jar with an airtight lid. Shake it until well combined. Set it aside.

To make the salad, start with a base of spring mix. Top it with the beets, shallot, tomatoes and Halloumi. Sprinkle the salad with the hemp hearts and drizzle it with the vinaigrette.

ROASTED POTATO SALAD WITH SAHAWIQ (SPICY CILANTRO SAUCE)

Sahawiq, also known as zhug, *is a spicy Yemeni condiment that combines cilantro with chile peppers and fragrant spices resulting in an scrumptious sauce. I paired it with roasted fingerling potatoes for their mild sweetness and creaminess, roasted celery for its unique herbaceous savoriness, red onion for its pungent sharpness and spinach for a pop of brightness. This salad is a fun little upgrade to your average potato salad and a great Middle Eastern addition to summer picnics.*

YIELD: 2 TO 3 SERVINGS

For the Potato Salad

1½ lb (680 g) baby or fingerling potatoes, sliced into rounds

2–3 ribs celery, chopped

1 tbsp (15 ml) extra virgin olive oil

1 tsp sea salt

2½ cups (70 g) chopped spinach

⅓ cup (55 g) chopped red onion

1 small red chile pepper, chopped (optional)

3 tbsp (25 g) toasted pine nuts

½ tsp Aleppo pepper

For the Sahawiq

2 large bunches cilantro (about 4 cups [65 g])

¼ cup (25 g) fresh mint leaves

1 medium jalapeño

2 medium cloves garlic, peeled

⅓ cup (80 ml) extra virgin olive oil

3 tbsp (45 ml) lime juice

1 tsp ground cumin

1 tsp ground coriander

1 tsp ground caraway

½ tsp ground cardamom

1 tsp sea salt

Preheat the oven to 400°F (205°C).

In a large bowl, combine the baby potatoes, celery, olive oil and salt. Mix the ingredients together until the veggies are well coated in oil and salt. Transfer them to a sheet pan. Bake, stirring once halfway through, until the potatoes are crispy on the outside and soft on the inside, about 25 minutes. Remove the sheet pan from the oven, and let the vegetables cool to room temperature.

To make the sahawiq, add the cilantro, mint, jalapeño, garlic, olive oil, lime juice, cumin, coriander, caraway, cardamom and salt to a food processor. Pulse it until completely smooth and creamy.

In a large bowl, mix together the roasted potatoes and celery with the spinach, onion, chile pepper (if using) and three-quarters of the sahawiq. Gently stir until well incorporated.

Serve at room temperature or chilled topped with pine nuts and Aleppo pepper with the remaining sahawiq on the side.

FREEKEH–MEDJOOL DATE SALAD WITH PRESERVED LEMON DRESSING

This salad combines everything I love about Middle Eastern and vegan cooking, and it is as far away from boring as it's possible to get. It combines freekeh/freek, a whole grain made from unripe durum wheat, with perfectly roasted cauliflower, peppery arugula and a sweet and intensely savory date and sun-dried tomato salsa. The salad is drizzled with a chia seed–preserved lemon dressing that's equal parts sour, salty and crunchy. I used North African, Levantine and Arabian Peninsula ingredients here to show how homogeneous various Middle Eastern cuisines can be, and this salad has become a mainstay in my household ever since.

YIELD: 3 TO 4 SERVINGS

For the Salad

3 cups (100 g) cauliflower florets

1 tbsp (15 ml) olive oil

½ tsp sea salt

1 cup (165 g) coarse freekeh, rinsed

1 cube vegetable bouillon

3 cups (60 g) arugula

Pine nuts, to serve

For the Salsa

5 jumbo Medjool dates, pitted and chopped

⅓ cup (60 g) jarred sun-dried tomatoes, chopped (a little oil is fine)

1 small shallot, chopped

¼ cup (15 g) chopped fresh parsley

6 medium green olives, pitted and chopped

1 small serrano pepper, chopped (optional)

3 tbsp (45 ml) lime juice

½ tsp sea salt

Preheat the oven to 400°F (205°C) and line a sheet pan with parchment paper.

In a large bowl, combine the cauliflower, olive oil and salt. Mix well and transfer it to the sheet pan. Roast, flipping once halfway through, until golden and crispy, about 25 minutes. Remove the sheet pan from the oven, and let the cauliflower cool to room temperature.

In a medium pot, combine the freekeh, bouillon and 2¼ cups (540 ml) of water. Bring it to a boil, then lower the heat to a simmer and cook until all or most of the water has been absorbed and freekeh has softened, 35 to 40 minutes. Drain any leftover water; the freekeh should be a bit chewy, similar to barley or brown rice. Remove it from the heat and let it cool to room temperature.

To make the salsa, place the dates, sun-dried tomatoes, shallot, parsley, olives, serrano pepper (if using), lime juice and salt in a medium bowl. Mix well to combine. Set it aside.

(continued)

For the Dressing

¼ cup (60 ml) extra virgin olive oil

1 preserved lemon, seeded and halved

1 tbsp (15 ml) preserved lemon brine

1 tbsp (15 ml) lemon juice

1 tbsp (15 ml) maple syrup

1 tbsp (2 g) fresh thyme leaves (or sub 1 tsp dried thyme)

1 tsp black pepper

1 tsp sea salt

1 tbsp (10 g) chia seeds

To make the dressing, add the extra virgin olive oil, preserved lemon, lemon brine, lemon juice, maple syrup, thyme, black pepper and salt to a food processor. Pulse it until smooth and creamy. Transfer the dressing to a jar with an airtight lid and stir in the chia seeds. Refrigerate any leftovers for up to 5 days.

Combine the cooked freekeh, roasted cauliflower and arugula in a large bowl along with half the dressing. Toss the ingredients to mix. Serve at room temperature topped with the salsa and a handful of pine nuts and with extra dressing on the side.

PANFRIED "CHICKEN" SALAD WITH SAVORY GRANOLA AND CILANTRO-PISTACHIO DRESSING

Nuts, seeds and spices play a huge role in Middle Eastern cuisine(s) so I created this savory granola to celebrate them. From pistachios and almonds to nigella seeds—called Seeds of Blessings in Arabic—to za'atar and sumac, the granola and the dressing both pay homage to the flavors of various regions and add that unique Middle Eastern flare to this simple "chicken" salad.

YIELD: 2 SALADS/ABOUT 2 CUPS (244 G) OF GRANOLA

For the Savory Granola

1 cup (80 g) old-fashioned oats

¾ cup (100–110 g) nuts of choice, roughly chopped (I used equal parts almonds, pistachios and cashews)

¼ cup (69 g) pumpkin seeds

2 tbsp (30 ml) olive oil

2 tbsp (9 g) nutritional yeast

1 tbsp (15 ml) maple syrup

1 tbsp (9 g) nigella seeds

1 tbsp (7 g) za'atar

1 tsp sumac

1 tsp garlic powder

1 tsp sea salt

For the Dressing

½ cup (8 g) fresh cilantro

¼ cup (60 ml) lemon juice

2 tbsp (32 g) pistachio butter

2 tbsp (30 ml) olive oil

2 tbsp (30 ml) grapevine brine or olive brine (from a jar)

1 small jalapeño

1 medium clove garlic, peeled

½ tsp sea salt

To make the savory granola, preheat the oven to 290°F (143°C).

To a large bowl, add the oats, nuts, pumpkin seeds, olive oil, nutritional yeast, maple syrup, nigella seeds, za'atar, sumac, garlic powder and salt. Mix well to thoroughly combine, then transfer the mixture to a sheet pan. Bake it for 30 to 35 minutes, or until lightly golden. Allow the granola to cool to room temperature before using, and store leftovers in an airtight container for up to 3 weeks.

To make the dressing, add the cilantro, lemon juice, pistachio butter, olive oil, brine, jalapeño, garlic and salt and to a food processor. Pulse it until completely smooth and creamy. Use immediately or refrigerate in an airtight container for up to 3 days.

(continued)

PANFRIED "CHICKEN" SALAD WITH SAVORY GRANOLA AND CILANTRO-PISTACHIO DRESSING (CONT.)

For the Salad

1½ Juicy "Chicken" breasts (page 24), sliced into strips

2 tbsp (30 ml) neutral oil

2 cups (134 g) chopped kale, stems removed

1 tsp extra virgin olive oil

½ tsp sea salt

2 cups (85 g) chopped spring mix

½ cup (75 g) sliced cherry tomatoes

1 small red onion, sliced

2 yellow sweet mini bell peppers, sliced

1 scallion, sliced

To prepare the chicken, heat the neutral oil over medium heat in a large skillet. Once shimmery, add the chicken strips and cook them until golden on all sides, about 2 minutes per side. Set them aside.

To prepare the greens, place the kale in a large bowl. Add the extra virgin olive oil and salt. Massage for 1 to 2 minutes, or until tender, then add the spring mix. Toss to combine.

To serve, start with a base of the kale and spring mix. Add the tomatoes, onion, bell peppers and cooked chicken. Top the salad with the scallion, savory granola and small dollops of the dressing. Serve immediately with extra dressing on the side.

IRRESISTIBLE SNACKS AND STARTERS

There's a reason the best known and most widely available Middle Eastern snack/starter is hummus. It's rich and creamy yet light and refreshing, and it is so incredibly versatile. While I absolutely love hummus and have included it here, Middle Eastern dips and starters go way beyond it. That's why Mezze platters—which are essentially the Middle Eastern equivalent to charcuterie boards—exist: They typically feature a selection of dips, salads, fresh and pickled veggies so you can experience the abundance of the region's appetizers.

Whenever someone asks me to introduce them to Middle Eastern food, I always start by serving dips. They're so unique and yet highly accessible. Plus, nothing compares to the pure and simple joy of loading pita bread with smooth and creamy deliciousness. Recipes such as my Baba Ghanouj (page 123), Sun-Dried Tomato Muhammara (page 127) and Mechouia-Inspired Roasted Mixed Pepper and Carrot Dip (page 138) are always highly requested and promptly devoured. Which isn't to say that other types of appetizers aren't just as incredible. The Kosa Bachamel Puff Pastry Cups (page 137), for instance, are saucy, flaky and perfect as a more elegant option, and the Batata Harra–Inspired Root Vegetables (page 128) are the definition of comfort food.

Back home, it's not uncommon to create a whole meal by serving a few of the starters featured here together—with a side of pita bread, of course. It's honestly my favorite kind of meal. I recommend you give it a shot, and I guarantee it will be epic!

BABA GHANOUJ (SMOKY EGGPLANT DIP)

For a big part of my life, I was a casual cook. I could throw together a dinner in a pinch, but I didn't have any specific recipes. Baba ghanouj was one of the first recipes I mastered, largely because I couldn't find a store-bought version in the United States that measured up to the ones I'd get from Middle Eastern restaurants back home. I must have made at least a dozen versions before I was satisfied with my recipe, and I have made a few more alterations which is why I'm so excited to share it. This version is smoky, garlicky, zesty, creamy and packed full of that specific savoriness unique to perfectly prepared eggplant. Aside from serving it as a dip, it pairs wonderfully with Hawawshi (page 73), Kebabs (page 64) and most roasted veggies. Fun fact: The term baba ghanouj *means "spoiled daddy."*

YIELD: ABOUT 2 CUPS (500 G)

For the Dip

2 large eggplants, halved

2 medium cloves garlic, peeled

1 tsp neutral oil

⅓ cup (80 g) tahini

3 tbsp (45 ml) lemon juice

2 tbsp (30 ml) olive oil, plus more for topping

1 tsp smoked paprika, plus more for topping

1 tsp sea salt, plus more if needed

To Serve

Chopped fresh parsley

The Best Pita Bread (page 19), toasted

Preheat the oven to 420°F (215°C) and line a sheet pan with parchment paper.

To make the dip, brush the eggplant and garlic with the neutral oil and transfer them to the sheet pan. Roast the garlic until soft and golden on both sides, flipping once halfway through, 15 to 20 minutes. Roast the eggplant until the flesh is golden and completely softened, flipping once halfway through, about 40 minutes. Remove the sheet pan from the oven, and let the eggplant cool completely.

Using a spoon, scoop out the eggplant flesh and place it in a food processor. Discard the skins. Add the roasted garlic, tahini, lemon juice, olive oil, smoked paprika and salt. Pulse it on high until completely smooth and creamy. Taste the baba ghanouj and add more salt if necessary.

Serve the baba ghanouj at room temperature or chilled topped with olive oil, smoked paprika and parsley with a side of toasted pita for dipping. Store leftovers in the refrigerator in an airtight container for up to 1 week.

DECONSTRUCTED SAMBOOSA (WHIPPED "FETA" DIP WITH SAMBOOSA SHELL CHIPS)

Samboosa, also known as sambousek*, is a beloved Middle Eastern appetizer, particularly popular during the month of Ramadan. It is similar to the Indian samosas or Chinese wontons. Samboosa is made of a thin rectangular pastry sheet stuffed with either herbed white cheese or spiced minced meat. Then it is rolled into a triangular pocket and fried to golden perfection. I prefer to control my own filling-to-pastry ratio, so I created this deconstructed version similar to chips and salsa. The whipped "feta" in this recipe is one I've worked on for a while, and I honestly think the final result is the tastiest and closest to actual Middle Eastern feta that I've had: salty, creamy, light and airy with understated but distinct notes of herbs and sourness. I paired it with chips made out of samboosa pastry and every single bite is reminiscent of the original with a little something extra.*

YIELD: 2 TO 3 SERVINGS

For the Whipped "Feta"

1 (16-oz [454-g]) block firm tofu

2 tbsp (30 ml) olive oil, plus extra for topping

1½ tbsp (8 g) nutritional yeast

1 tbsp (15 g) tahini

1 tbsp (18 g) white miso

1 tbsp (15 ml) apple cider vinegar

1 tbsp (15 ml) lemon juice

1 tbsp (15 ml) vegan cooking cream (optional)

½ tsp garlic powder

½ tsp onion powder

1 tsp sea salt

1 small bunch mint, finely chopped

Nigella seeds

White sesame seeds

Toasted cumin seeds

Dried parsley

Dried mint

Aleppo pepper

For the Samboosa Chips

10–12 samboosa sheets, sliced diagonally into triangles

¼–½ cup (60–120 ml) neutral oil

To make the "feta," place the tofu in a tofu press. Alternatively, wrap it in a kitchen towel and place a heavy object, such as a cast-iron skillet, on top. Let it sit for 30 minutes to release extra moisture.

Once done, pat the tofu dry. Place it in a food processor with the olive oil, nutritional yeast, tahini, miso, vinegar, lemon juice, cooking cream (if using), garlic powder, onion powder and salt. Pulse it until smooth and creamy.

Transfer the mixture to a large bowl. Using a hand mixer at medium speed, whip up the "feta" until light, airy and fluffy. Transfer it to a serving bowl. Fold in the fresh mint and top it with olive oil, a sprinkling of nigella, sesame and toasted cumin seeds, dried parsley, dried mint and Aleppo pepper. Refrigerate the "feta" while you prepare the chips.

To make the samboosa chips, line a plate with a paper towel. Heat the neutral oil in a large skillet over medium-low heat. Once shimmery, add the samboosa triangles and fry them until just lightly golden, 30 to 40 seconds. They will continue to cook and darken in color as they cool. Transfer to the plate. Once all the chips are fried, serve them immediately along with the chilled whipped "feta" dip.

SUN-DRIED TOMATO MUHAMMARA (WALNUT-PEPPER-POMEGRANATE DIP)

This recipe started out as a challenge of sorts because my husband didn't think there was any conceivable way of improving classic muhammara. *In case you're unfamiliar with it, muhammara is a Levantine dip made of toasted walnuts, roasted red bell pepper, pomegranate molasses and tahini. It's rich, tangy, creamy, slightly sweet and beautifully earthy. I decided to boost its savoriness and tanginess with the addition of sun-dried tomatoes and, despite his earlier skepticism, my husband was impressed and I was too. This muhammara makes a great addition to charcuterie and grazing boards, as a stand-alone appetizer and even as a sandwich spread.*

YIELD: 2 TO 3 SERVINGS

For the Dip

1 cup (117 g) walnuts, whole or pieces

1 large red bell pepper, seeded, roasted and peeled

½ cup (54 g) plain, vegan bread crumbs

½ cup (90 g) jarred sun-dried tomatoes (a little oil is fine)

1 large clove garlic, peeled

¼ cup (60 ml) lemon juice

2 tbsp (30 ml) extra virgin olive oil

2 tbsp (40 g) pomegranate molasses

1½ tbsp (23 g) tahini

1 tbsp (15 ml) agave or maple syrup

1 tsp Aleppo pepper

1 tsp sea salt

To Serve

1 tsp sun-dried tomatoes oil marinade (from the jar)

Chopped fresh parsley

Pinch of Aleppo pepper

Crackers or raw veggies of choice

To make the dip, heat a medium skillet over medium-high heat until hot and lightly smoking. Add the walnuts and toast them, stirring frequently, until fragrant and lightly golden, 2 to 3 minutes. Watch them closely to be sure they cook evenly and to avoid scorching. Remove the skillet from the heat, and let the walnuts cool to room temperature.

In a food processor, combine the toasted walnuts, bell pepper, bread crumbs, sun-dried tomatoes, garlic, lemon juice, olive oil, pomegranate molasses, tahini, agave, Aleppo pepper and salt. Pulse it, stopping to scrape down the sides as needed, until completely smooth and creamy.

Refrigerate the dip for 1 hour or enjoy at room temperature. To serve, plate the muhammara, then drizzle with sun-dried tomato oil and top with parsley and Aleppo pepper. Pair with your favorite crackers and/or raw veggies.

BATATA HARRA–INSPIRED ROOT VEGETABLES

Batata Harra *translates to "spicy potatoes," and it is a popular Levantine dish of hot and sour fried potatoes. While I love the original, I decided to substitute the potatoes with root veggies—which I think are seriously underrated—to show how delectable they can be. I also chose to roast my veggies because I find that the freshness of batata harra can often be bogged down by greasiness. This spicy, garlicky, zesty dish will have even the pickiest of eaters coming back for more.*

YIELD: 4 TO 5 SERVINGS

For the Vegetables

3 medium red beets, peeled and rinsed

3 medium golden beets, peeled and rinsed

2 medium turnips, peeled, rinsed and cubed

3 tbsp (45 ml) neutral oil, divided

2 tsp (10 g) sea salt, divided

3 medium sweet potatoes, peeled, rinsed and cubed

2 tbsp (30 ml) olive oil

4 medium cloves garlic, minced

1 large bunch fresh parsley, finely chopped

1 large bunch fresh cilantro, finely chopped

1 tsp smoked paprika

1 tsp red pepper flakes

4 tbsp (60 ml) lemon juice, divided

To make the vegetables, place the red beets in a medium-sized pot, cover them with water and bring it to a boil. Cook until fork tender but not mushy, about 1 hour. Remove the pot from the heat. Rinse the beets under cold water, then transfer them to a medium bowl and allow them to cool to room temperature.

Follow the same steps for the golden beets. Be sure to cook separately otherwise the red beets will stain the golden ones. This step can be done the night before. Just refrigerate the cooked golden and red beets separately, each in an airtight container until ready to use.

Preheat the oven to 420°F (215°C).

In a large bowl, add the turnips, 1 tablespoon (15 ml) of neutral oil and ½ teaspoon of salt. Stir until the turnips are well coated. Transfer them to a sheet pan—don't overcrowd. Roast for 25 minutes, flip, then roast for 20 minutes, or until fork tender and golden on both sides. Set them aside.

In the same bowl used for the turnips, combine the sweet potatoes with 1 tablespoon (15 ml) of neutral oil and the remaining ½ teaspoon of salt. Stir until the sweet potatoes are well coated and transfer them to a sheet pan. Roast the potatoes for 20 minutes, flip, then roast for 15 minutes, or until lightly charred at the edges and crispy. Set them aside.

Chop the steamed red and golden beets into cubes similar in size to the turnips and sweet potatoes. Place the golden beet cubes in the bowl used for the other veggies, add 1 tablespoon (15 ml) of neutral oil and mix well. Place the beets on a sheet pan and roast for 8 minutes, flip, and roast for 8 minutes, or until lightly crisped on both sides. Follow the same steps for the red beets and set both aside.

Heat the olive oil in a large pan over medium heat. Once shimmery, add the garlic and cook for 1 minute, stirring to prevent burning, until lightly golden. Add the parsley, cilantro, smoked paprika, red pepper flakes and 1 teaspoon of salt. Continue to stir for 1 minute, or until the herbs have shrunk in size and are a vibrant green. Transfer one-quarter of the mixture to a small bowl and set that bowl aside.

(continued)

BATATA HARRA–INSPIRED ROOT VEGETABLES (CONT.)

To Serve
Handful fresh parsley leaves
Lemon wedges

Add the turnips, sweet potatoes and golden beets to the pan, and stir for 30 seconds to warm them. Remove the pan from the heat. Stir in 3 tablespoons (45 ml) of lemon juice and mix well.

Meanwhile, add the red beets to the bowl containing the one-quarter of the mixture you set aside. Add the remaining 1 tablespoon (15 ml) of lemon juice and mix well. This is to prevent the red beets from staining the other veggies.

Plate the root veggies and distribute the red beets among them. Top with parsley and a side of lemon wedges.

HUMMUS THREE WAYS MEZZE PLATTER

Hummus boards are one of my favorite appetizers to make and eat. The base components of hummus—chickpeas and tahini—are incredibly versatile, which makes it easy to add other ingredients and end up with very different flavor profiles. For this board I made roasted garlic preserved lemon hummus (earthy and sour), harissa roasted pepper hummus (spicy and sweet) and parsley dill hummus (fresh and herbaceous). I paired the hummus with dipping-friendly veggies, nuts, pickles, crackers and chips for a visually enticing and nutritious platter that's perfect for entertaining.

YIELD: ABOUT 2 CUPS (500 G) OF EACH HUMMUS

For the Hummus Base

1½ cups (246 g) cooked chickpeas

⅓ cup (80 g) tahini

3 tbsp (45 ml) extra virgin olive oil, plus more for topping

2 tbsp (30 ml) lemon juice

For the Roasted Garlic Preserved Lemon Hummus

8 medium cloves garlic, roasted

1 large preserved lemon, pulp scraped out

2 tbsp (30 ml) preserved lemon brine

½ tsp sea salt

Cooked chickpeas, to serve

Fresh cilantro microgreens or chopped cilantro, to serve

Hemp hearts, to serve

For the Harissa Roasted Pepper Hummus

1 large roasted red bell pepper, peeled and seeded

2 tbsp (30 g) harissa paste

1 tsp smoked paprika, plus more to serve

1 tsp sea salt

Aleppo pepper, to serve

To make the roasted garlic preserved lemon hummus, place the base ingredients of cooked chickpeas, tahini, olive oil and lemon juice along with the roasted garlic, preserved lemon and preserved lemon brine and salt in a food processor with ¼ cup (60 ml) of cold water. Pulse it until completely smooth and creamy. There may be slight variations in texture based on the type of tahini and the consistency of the ingredients used. The rule of thumb is to add more tahini if the hummus is too thin and more water if it's too thick. Transfer it to a bowl and top with the cooked chickpeas, cilantro and hemp hearts.

To make the harissa roasted pepper hummus, place the base ingredients of cooked chickpeas, tahini, olive oil and lemon juice along with the roasted red bell pepper, harissa paste, smoked paprika and salt in a food processor with ¼ cup (60 ml) of cold water. Pulse it until completely smooth and creamy, transfer it to a bowl and top with more smoked paprika and Aleppo pepper.

(continued)

HUMMUS THREE WAYS MEZZE PLATTER (CONT.)

For the Parsley Dill Hummus

¾ cup (45 g) fresh parsley

⅓ cup (16 g) fresh dill

2 tbsp (6 g) fresh chives

1 tbsp (15 ml) lemon juice

1 tsp sea salt

Nigella seeds, to serve

To Serve

Fresh vegetables, such as cherry tomatoes, cucumber spears and mini sweet bell peppers, for dipping

Pickles of choice, such as baby cucumbers and pepperoncinis

Smoked pistachios or nuts of choice

Steamed edamame

Chips and crackers, for dipping

To make the parsley dill hummus, place the base ingredients of cooked chickpeas, tahini, olive oil and lemon juice along with the parsley, dill, chives, additional lemon juice and salt with ¼ cup (60 ml) of cold water. Pulse it until completely smooth and creamy, transfer it to a bowl and top it with the nigella seeds.

To serve, place all the ingredients on a large platter. Hummus can be served at room temperature or cold, and it can be refrigerated for up to 1 week in an airtight container.

SALATA ASWAD (EGGPLANT–PEANUT BUTTER DIP)

While peanut butter isn't an ingredient that typically comes to mind when one thinks of Middle Eastern food, it's actually pretty common in Sudan. In fact, the Arabic term for peanuts, which are actually legumes, is "Sundanese beans" because of how prevalent they are in Sudanese cuisine and as a Sudanese export. This dip combines peanut butter with aswad *(eggplant) and tomatoes for an umami-bomb of an appetizer. While many versions use fried eggplant, I find that roasted eggplant results in a smokier, less greasy dish, and it allows the robust peanut butter flavor to fully shine through.*

YIELD: 2 SERVINGS

1 large eggplant, halved

1 tbsp (15 ml) olive oil

1 tbsp (15 ml) neutral oil

1 small onion, finely chopped

1 small jalapeño, finely chopped (optional)

1 large clove garlic, minced

1 tbsp (16 g) tomato paste

1 cup (180 g) grape or Campari tomatoes, finely chopped

½ tsp ground cumin

1 tsp sea salt

2 tbsp (32 g) peanut butter

1 tbsp (15 ml) lemon juice

Pita bread and/or crackers, for dipping

Preheat the oven to 420°F (215°C) and line a sheet pan with parchment paper.

Brush the eggplant with the olive oil and transfer them to the sheet pan. Roast the eggplant until the flesh is golden and completely softened, flipping once halfway through, about 40 minutes. Remove the sheet pan from the oven, and let the eggplant cool completely. When cool, scoop out the eggplant flesh, discard the skins and roughly chop the flesh. Set it aside.

Heat the neutral oil in a large skillet over medium heat. Once shimmery, add the onion and cook until translucent and golden at the edges, about 5 minutes. Add the jalapeño (if using) and garlic. Cook, stirring, until the garlic is fragrant and is just starting to darken in color, 1 to 2 minutes.

Reduce the heat to medium-low and add the tomato paste. Using a spatula, flatten and break apart the tomato paste while mixing with the vegetables until softened and slightly darker in color, 1 to 2 minutes. This results in a deeper umami flavor.

Add the tomatoes, cumin and salt. Mix well. Cook until the tomatoes have wilted and broken apart, about 5 minutes. Stir in the peanut butter and mix until well incorporated. Add the roasted eggplant. Continue cooking, stirring occasionally, until the mixture is creamy and chunky, about 5 minutes. Remove the skillet from the heat and stir in the lemon juice. Serve the salata warm, at room temperature or chilled with pita bread and/or crackers.

KOSA BACHAMEL (ZUCCHINI BÉCHAMEL CASSEROLE) PUFF PASTRY CUPS

These cups are a play on kosa bel bachamel, *a delectable Egyptian casserole reminiscent of lasagna, that's made by layering steamed kosa (zucchini), ground beef and béchamel—a French roux and milk sauce similar to Alfredo. I've been wanting to transform the dish into an appetizer by giving it a lighter and fresher makeover, which is how this recipe came to be. I used puff pastry cups baked to golden perfection, stuffed them with crispy vegan grounds and thin strips of zucchini and drizzled them with vegan béchamel. Each bite delivers the delightful flavors of the casserole co-cooned in sinfully flaky pastry.*

YIELD: 6 PUFF PASTRY CUPS

For the Puff Pastry Cups

1 tbsp (15 ml) neutral oil

1 small onion, chopped

6 oz (170 g) vegan sausage, crumbled

1 small tomato, chopped (I used Campari)

1 tbsp (8 g) pine nuts

½ tsp ground cinnamon

½ tsp sea salt

1 small zucchini, shaved into sheets

6 (10 oz [283 g]) vegan puff pastry shells, baked according to package instructions

For the Bachamel

2 tbsp (28 g) vegan butter

1½ tbsp (12 g) all-purpose flour

1 cup (240 ml) unsweetened plant milk

½ tsp ground nutmeg

½ tsp black pepper

¾ tsp sea salt

To Serve

Fresh oregano leaves

Aleppo pepper

To make the puff pastry cups, heat the oil in a medium skillet over medium heat. Once shimmery, add the onion and cook until softened and golden, about 8 minutes. Add the sausage and cook, occasionally stirring, until the sausage is crispy and browned, about 7 minutes. Add the tomato and cook for 2 minutes. Add the pine nuts, cinnamon and salt. Cook for 1 minute, or until the tomato breaks down. Remove the skillet from the heat, and let the mixture cool for 10 minutes.

To make the bachamel, melt the vegan butter in a small pot over medium heat. Once bubbling, add the flour. Whisk together the flour the whole time to evenly cook and avoid scorching until golden in color, about 2 minutes. Add the milk, nutmeg, black pepper and salt. Continue whisking to avoid the sauce getting lumpy until the sauce has thickened to the consistency of a light gravy, 3 to 5 minutes. It will thicken more as it cools. Remove the pot from the heat and set it aside.

Fold a sheet of zucchini into whatever shape best suits your puff pastry shell. Add the sausage filling. Top each puff pastry cup with a couple of oregano leaves, sprinkle with Aleppo pepper, drizzle with a teaspoon of bachamel and serve the rest of the sauce on the side.

MECHOUIA-INSPIRED ROASTED MIXED PEPPER AND CARROT DIP

This recipe was inspired by Tunisian salata mechouia, *a salad typically made by mashing together grilled veggies then adding canned tuna and hard-boiled eggs. My recipe shares many of mechouia's core ingredients, but ultimately it's quite different and features flavors from other North African regions and the Levant. This dip combines roasted veggies—charred just enough to add that delectable caramelized savoriness—with tahini, turmeric and harissa, all whipped up into a fluffy sweet and spicy concoction. I usually make this when I have an overabundance of peppers from my garden in late summer and early fall, and it's almost always immediately wiped out.*

YIELD: 4 SERVINGS

For the Dip

1 lb (454 g) carrots, peeled and roughly chopped

1 medium red bell pepper, roughly chopped

1 medium green bell pepper, roughly chopped

1 medium yellow bell pepper, roughly chopped

1 medium orange bell pepper, roughly chopped

3 mini sweet red bell peppers, roughly chopped

1 serrano pepper, halved (optional)

2 jalapeños, halved (seeded if you prefer less spice)

3 ribs celery, roughly chopped

1 large onion, quartered

6 medium cloves garlic, peeled

3 tbsp (45 ml) neutral oil

2 tbsp (30 g) tahini

2 tbsp (30 g) harissa paste

1 tsp ground turmeric

2 tsp (10 g) sea salt

To Serve

Olive oil

Pine nuts

Pumpkin seeds

Smoked paprika

Preheat the oven to 400°F (205°C) and line two sheet pans with parchment paper.

To make the dip, combine the carrots, all the peppers, celery, onion and garlic with the neutral oil in a large bowl. Mix well to combine. Transfer the mixture to the sheet pans and roast, flipping once or twice to evenly cook, until the vegetables are softened and lightly charred, about 40 minutes. Remove the sheet pans from the oven, and let the vegetables cool to room temperature.

In a food processor, combine the roasted vegetables with the tahini, harissa paste, turmeric and salt. Pulse it until completely smooth and creamy. Serve the dip at room temperature or chilled topped with olive oil, pine nuts, pumpkin seeds and smoked paprika. Refrigerate leftovers in an airtight container for up to 1 week.

KIBBEH NAYEH (RAW BULGUR, NUT AND HERB SPREAD)

This plant-based take on kibbeh nayeh, *or raw kibbeh, is one that originated within the Middle Eastern Christian community for Lent, the 40-day fasting period preceding Easter. It's also another one that was inspired by cookbook author Reem Kassis's version, though I changed the nuts and I added sun-dried tomatoes and a wider selection of herbs for more of a flavor punch. Though kibbeh nayeh is a recent discovery of mine, it has quickly become a favorite.*

YIELD: 4 SERVINGS

For the Spread

⅓ cup (39 g) walnuts

⅓ cup (48 g) almonds

1 cup (175 g) fine bulgur wheat

⅓ cup (60 g) jarred sun-dried tomatoes

3 medium Campari or 2 medium Roma tomatoes, halved

1 large shallot, peeled and halved

1 medium jalapeño or serrano pepper, halved

¼ cup (60 ml) extra virgin olive oil, plus more for drizzling

1 tbsp (16 g) tomato paste

1 tbsp (20 g) pomegranate molasses

1 tbsp (5 g) nutritional yeast

2 tsp (4 g) smoked paprika

1 tsp sumac

1 tsp ground coriander

1 tsp dried marjoram

1 tsp dried mint

1 tsp ground cumin

1 tsp sea salt, or more to taste

To Serve

Aleppo pepper

Chopped arugula microgreens or chopped fresh parsley

Iceberg lettuce leaves

Toasted bread of choice

To make the spread, heat a medium skillet over high heat. Once it's smoking, add the walnuts and almonds and cook, stirring frequently to prevent burning, until fragrant and toasted, about 4 minutes. Remove the skillet from the heat, transfer the nuts to a plate and let them cool completely. When cool, place the walnuts and almonds in a food processor and pulse it until coarsely ground, but not powdered or buttery. Set them aside.

In a large bowl, combine the bulgur wheat with 1¼ cups (295 ml) of boiling water. Mix well and cover until the water is fully absorbed, around 10 minutes. Fluff, cover again and refrigerate until completely cooled.

To a food processor, add the sun-dried tomatoes, tomatoes, shallot, jalapeño, olive oil, tomato paste, pomegranate molasses, nutritional yeast, smoked paprika, sumac, coriander, marjoram, mint, cumin and salt. Pulse it until completely smooth.

Add the processed mixture and coarsely ground nuts to the bulgur wheat. Mix by hand until the kibbeh is well incorporated and has a firm but malleable texture that is neither wet nor crumbly. Serve chilled or at room temperature drizzled with olive oil and sprinkled with Aleppo pepper and microgreens with a side of lettuce leaves and/or toasted bread for dipping/spreading.

DELECTABLE DESSERTS

I've never been a fan of making desserts, and most days I'd go for a candy bar rather than deal with the countless sticky measuring cups, the floury surfaces and the stress of getting the precise cook time right. I do, however, get nostalgic for Middle Eastern desserts every once in a while, and finding them where I live is next to impossible. Which is why I've developed a small, but incredibly satisfying arsenal of easy, sinfully scrumptious Middle Eastern dessert recipes that I'm stoked to share with you!

This chapter can be divided into two sections. The first three recipes are whole food–based breakfast options that can also double as sweet treats. The Cardamom, Orange and Peanut Granola (page 149) is loaded with nutrient-dense ingredients, but still tastes surprisingly similar to Egyptian orange cake. And the Rose Water–Chia Pudding (page 146) is so subtly sweet and fragrant you'll feel as though you've stepped into a Middle Eastern apothecary.

The latter five recipes are rich, enticing masterpieces that fully embrace the decadence of Middle Eastern desserts. These were probably the hardest to veganize: I had to test some of the recipes more times than you'd believe to achieve results that worked, were easy to reproduce and tasted just like the originals. I'm very happy to say I did it though. I'm particularly proud of the Basbousa (page 153), which is just as buttery and pleasantly crumbly as its non-vegan counterpart and the Walnut Pecan Baklava (page 154), which is so crisp and flaky it's worth every minute of the layering process.

Every recipe is this section uses ingredients that have been part of Middle Eastern cuisine for centuries, if not millennia, and my main aim was to do justice to that. I hope you love them as much as I do.

COCONUT AND PEANUT BUTTER STUFFED MEDJOOL DATES WITH TAHINI-MOLASSES DRIZZLE

Dates are a staple in Middle Eastern cuisine, particularly in the Arabian Peninsula, and are usually the first thing people will eat to break their fast during Ramadan. This recipe showcases the irresistible gooeyness of dates and pairs them with a beloved Egyptian combo: blackstrap molasses and tahini. This is a quick and easy recipe for whenever you're craving a dessert. It's great to make in batches and store in the fridge or freezer for a chewier caramel texture. I particularly enjoy these dates as a post-workout treat for a tasty energy booster.

YIELD: 16 DATES

16 large Medjool dates
¼ cup (64 g) peanut butter
½ cup (50 g) shredded coconut (sweetened or unsweetened)
2 tbsp (30 g) runny tahini
2 tbsp (40 g) blackstrap molasses
1 tsp dried rose petals (optional)
½ tsp flaky sea salt

Using a knife, cut the Medjool dates lengthwise and remove the pits. Gently spread them open. Divide the dates in half. Stuff half with the peanut butter and half with the shredded coconut. You could also stuff a few with a mixture of both peanut butter and coconut.

Optional step: Transfer them to a plate and place in the freezer for 15 minutes to give the dates a more caramel-like texture.

Drizzle the dates with the tahini and molasses, then sprinkle them with the rose petals (if using) and salt.

Serve the dates immediately or store them in a container at room temperature for up to 4 days, in the fridge for up to 2 weeks or in the freezer for up to 2 months. Let them thaw at room temperature for 10 to 15 minutes before eating.

ROSE WATER–CHIA PUDDING

If you're looking for a nutrient-packed, dessert-for-breakfast option that's bursting with Middle Eastern flavors and takes all of five minutes to prepare, this is the perfect recipe for you! This rose water–chia pudding is as delicious as it is fragrant. It was inspired by Roz bell laban, *Egyptian rice pudding. The texture of all the different layers—gooey chia pudding, creamy yogurt, crunchy walnuts, juicy fruits and fresh mint—makes it such a fun and unique breakfast treat. This chia pudding is also a great meal prep option: I'll usually make it in large batches and have jars of it in my fridge ready to go.*

YIELD: 4 SERVINGS

2 cups (480 ml) plant milk

¾ cup (122 g) chia seeds

1 tbsp (15 ml) maple syrup

¾ tbsp (11 ml) rose water

10.6 oz (300 g) vegan mango-peach yogurt or flavor of choice

Chopped walnuts or nuts of choice, to taste

Sliced fresh peaches and mangoes, to taste

Handful of mint leaves

To make the chia pudding, combine the plant milk, chia seeds, maple syrup, rose water and yogurt in a medium bowl. Mix it well, then divide the pudding between four small jars with airtight lids or bowls you can wrap with saran wrap. Refrigerate the pudding for at least 6 hours, or preferably overnight to set.

To serve, top with the walnuts, fresh peaches and mangoes and mint leaves. Serve chilled. Refrigerate any leftovers for up to 1 week.

CARDAMOM, ORANGE AND PEANUT GRANOLA

Ever since I learned how easy granola is to make, it's been a staple in my kitchen. I've tried a wide array of different ingredient pairings, but this one, in my opinion and according to my husband who's a granola fanatic, is the winner. The flavors of this granola were inspired by my grandmother's old-school Egyptian orange cake—easily one of my fondest childhood food memories—and the cardamom-forward Turkish coffee commonly served in the Arabian Peninsula. Every bite of this granola is packed with notes of citrus, spice and nuts and is equally enjoyable with or without milk.

YIELD: ABOUT 16 SERVINGS

5 cups (400 g) whole grain old-fashioned oats

¾ cup (194 g) peanut butter

½ cup (120 ml) maple syrup or agave

1 large orange, zested and juiced

½ cup (58 g) chopped hazelnuts or nuts of choice

½ cup (56 g) chopped macadamia nuts or nuts of choice

1 tbsp (15 ml) orange blossom water

1 tbsp (9 g) white sesame seeds

1 tbsp (9 g) poppy seeds

1 tbsp (8 g) amaranth (optional)

½ tbsp (4 g) ground cinnamon

½ tsp ground cardamom

½ tsp sea salt

¼ cup (40 g) dark raisins

¼ cup (40 g) golden raisins

Preheat the oven to 280°F (138°C). Place one rack in the middle of your oven and one at the top.

In a large bowl, combine the oats, peanut butter, maple syrup, orange zest and juice, nuts, orange blossom water, sesame seeds, poppy seeds, amaranth (if using), cinnamon, cardamom and salt.

Stir just until all the ingredients are well mixed, but avoid overmixing if you want to form clusters. Divide the mixture between two large sheet pans and bake on the middle rack for 25 minutes. If your pans don't fit on one rack, place one on the middle rack and one on the upper rack, then switch them halfway through baking.

Transfer the sheet pans to the upper rack and bake for another 25 minutes, or until golden and crunchy. Check the granola often during the second half of the baking time to avoid burning it.

Let the granola cool completely before stirring in the raisins and transferring it to a large airtight container. Store the granola at room temperature for up to 1 month.

KLEICHA (DATE PASTRY)–INSPIRED DATE CINNAMON ROLLS

Kleicha is an Iraqi date cookie most often baked for religious holidays, and it's the inspiration for these decadent cinnamon rolls. The filling for my rolls is almost identical to that of kleicha—mine just has more cinnamon—but the main difference is in the dough. While kleicha is traditionally crumbly, I opted for a pillowy, fluffy texture. The date and cardamom flavors take the comfort level of these rolls to epic proportions, and they're even better with a mug of freshly brewed tea.

YIELD: 16 TO 20 ROLLS

For the Dough

2½ tsp (10 g) active dry yeast

2 tbsp (30 g) sugar

½ cup (120 ml) plus 2 tbsp (30 ml) butter, melted then cooled to room temperature, divided

¼ cup (60 ml) plant milk, at room temperature

1 tsp baking powder

¼ tsp sea salt

3 cups (375 g) all-purpose flour, plus more as needed and for dusting

½ tsp neutral oil

For the Filling

14–16 large Medjool dates, pitted

2 tbsp (14 g) ground cinnamon

½ tsp ground cardamom

Pinch of sea salt

To make the dough, whisk together the active dry yeast and sugar with ½ cup (120 ml) of warm water in a large bowl. Let the mixture sit until a foamy layer forms on the top indicating the yeast is active, 5 to 10 minutes.

Whisk in ½ cup (120 ml) of melted butter, milk, baking powder and salt. Once well incorporated, add 3 cups (375 g) of all-purpose flour and knead to combine. If the dough is too wet, add more flour 1 tablespoon (8 g) at a time until the dough no longer sticks to your hand but is still moist. Transfer the dough to a floured surface and continue kneading for 5 to 10 minutes, until the dough is elastic and moist, but not sticky or crumbly.

Grease a large, clean bowl with the oil then place the dough in it. Cover with a damp towel and set the bowl in a dark, warm spot until doubled in size, about 1 hour.

To make the filling, combine the dates, cinnamon, cardamom and salt with ¾ cup (180 ml) of hot water in a food processor. Pulse it until the dates are completely pulverized and you have a creamy, and spreadable caramel-like paste. Let it cool to room temperature.

Preheat the oven to 350°F (180°C) and line a sheet pan with parchment paper.

Transfer the risen dough to a floured surface and roll out into a 14 x 9–inch (35 x 23–cm) rectangle. Evenly spread the date filling over the dough, making sure to leave a ¼-inch (6-mm) margin at the edges.

Tightly roll the dough starting from the shorter side of the rectangle. Using a serrated knife, evenly divide the dough into 16 to 20 rolls. Place the rolls on the sheet pan either upright or laid down horizontally. Bake the rolls until lightly golden, 15 to 17 minutes depending on their size.

Remove them from the oven, brush them with the remaining 2 tablespoons (30 ml) of butter and transfer them to a cooling rack. Serve warm or at room temperature. Refrigerate leftovers in an airtight container for up to 10 days.

BASBOUSA (SEMOLINA CAKE)

While basbousa *is originally Egyptian, it can be found throughout virtually all of the Middle East. To* bess *in Arabic means "to dredge," which is where this dessert gets its name, because it's made by massaging butter into semolina granules before adding the rest of the ingredients. Creating a vegan version of basbousa that had the same rich-yet-light flavor and solid-yet-crumbly texture was tricky, but after much recipe testing, the result is breathtaking. Every bite is buttery, melt-in-your-mouth good and bursting with the gorgeous floral flavors of the soaking syrup. Fun fact, because of its sweetness,* basbousa *is used as a term of endearment between loved ones.*

YIELD: 20 TO 24 PIECES

For the Basbousa

3 cups (500 g) semolina, medium grind

1 cup (240 ml) vegan butter, melted and cooled to room temperature, plus 1 tsp for greasing

¾ cup (150 g) granulated sugar

½ cup (55 g) coconut flour, preferably coarse

½ cup (110 g) vegan sour cream

½ cup (115 g) plain vegan yogurt

1 tsp baking powder

¼-½ cup (60–120 ml) plant milk, at room temperature

20–24 almonds

For the Simple Syrup

2 cups (400 g) sugar

3 tbsp (45 ml) lemon juice, or more to taste

1 tbsp (15 g) vegan butter

1 tsp rose water

1 tsp blossom water

In a large bowl, combine the semolina and melted butter. Using your hands, massage the butter into the semolina until all the semolina granules look well coated/saturated. This ensures the basbousa has that lovely crumbly texture.

Add the sugar, coconut flour, sour cream, yogurt and baking powder to the semolina. Gently fold the ingredients in using a spatula until incorporated. Don't knead, vigorously stir or overmix because that will cause the texture to harden once baked.

Add ¼ cup (60 ml) of milk and fold it in. If the mixture is too dry, add another ¼ cup (60 ml) of milk. The texture should be similar to corn bread, wet but holding together. Cover and place the mixture in the fridge for 45 minutes.

To make the simple syrup, combine 2 cups (480 ml) of water with the sugar and lemon juice in a medium saucepan. Whisk it together to dissolve, then place the pan over high heat. Once boiling, let the mixture reduce for 15 minutes. Remove the saucepan from the heat and stir in the butter, rose water and blossom water. Whisk until the butter is completely dissolved. Set it aside.

Preheat the oven to 350°F (180°C) and grease the bottom and sides of a 9 x 13-inch (22 x 33–cm) cake pan with 1 teaspoon of butter.

Spread the chilled basbousa mixture evenly in the pan. Using a serrated knife, cut into either 20 or 24 squares. Press an almond in the center of each square. Bake the basbousa for 25 to 27 minutes, or until lightly golden at the edges. Broil for 5 to 7 minutes, or until top is crispy and golden.

Remove the pan from the oven and immediately ladle simple syrup onto it. Continue to add syrup one ladleful at a time until it stops being immediately absorbed. Serve the basbousa at room temperature with extra syrup on the side.

WALNUT PECAN BAKLAVA

Baklava is one of these desserts that can be found in most Middle Eastern cuisines, though it's not exclusive to the Middle East. It's available year-round, but most commonly served during Ramadan and religious feasts. Baklava is made by layering buttered sheets of very thin phyllo pastry and spiced nuts. As it bakes, the phyllo sheets separate and crisp up. The result is a splendidly flaky finished dish that's soaked in a lightly floral and citrusy syrup. Though not typically used in baklava, I paired buttery pecans with the traditional earthy walnuts, and the result was one irresistible dessert.

YIELD: 18 LARGE OR 24 MEDIUM PIECES

For the Syrup

1½ cups (300 g) granulated sugar

½ cup (120 ml) maple syrup

1 tbsp (15 ml) lemon juice

Peel of 1 medium orange

1 cinnamon stick

1 tsp rose water

For the Baklava

12 oz (340 g) walnuts

8 oz (227 g) pecans

1½ tbsp (12 g) ground cinnamon

1 tsp ground nutmeg

¼ tsp ground cardamom (optional)

1 cup (227 g) vegan butter, melted then cooled to room temperature, plus more for greasing

31 phyllo dough sheets (see Note)

NOTE: Baklava requires very thin phyllo dough sheets. Make sure you get #4 phyllo sheets (0.28 inches or 7 mm thickness).

To make the syrup, whisk together the sugar, maple syrup and lemon juice in a medium saucepan with 1 cup (240 ml) of water. Add the orange peel and cinnamon stick. Bring to a boil over medium-high heat. Reduce the heat to medium-low and simmer until thickened but still easily pourable, 12 to 15 minutes. Discard the orange peel and cinnamon stick. Stir in the rose water and set it aside.

Preheat the oven to 350°F (177°C).

To make the baklava, combine the walnuts, pecans, cinnamon, nutmeg and cardamom (if using) in a food processor. Pulse it until the nuts are coarsely crumbled. Set it aside.

Brush the bottom of a 9 x 13–inch (23 x 33–cm) pan with butter. Gently place a layer of phyllo. Phyllo is very delicate so don't worry about small rips because they'll be covered up as you layer. Brush the phyllo layer with a thin layer of butter, then add another layer of phyllo and brush again. Repeat until you've layered eight sheets of phyllo.

Once you've buttered the eighth layer, evenly spread one-quarter of the nut mixture. Repeat the process of buttering and layering five more sheets of phyllo. Spread another one-quarter of the nut mix, layer five more sheets of phyllo and repeat twice more. Once you've gotten to the last layer of nuts, top with eight layers of buttered phyllo. Brush the top layer as well.

All in all, it should be: eight sheets, nut layer, five sheets, nut layer, five sheets, nut layer, five sheets, nut layer, eight sheets.

Trim any messy looking edges, if needed. Using a sharp knife, gently cut the baklava into nine or twelve even squares, then diagonally slice each square for a total of 18 or 24 triangles. Bake the baklava until crispy and golden, 50 to 55 minutes.

Evenly ladle all the syrup onto the baklava as soon as you remove the baklava from the oven. Let it sit at room temperature for at least 2 hours uncovered or preferably overnight, loosely cover after the first 2 hours, to allow the syrup to soak in.

Store leftovers in an airtight container for up to 4 days at room temperature or refrigerate for up to 2 weeks.

PISTACHIO DATE CHEESECAKE

Cheesecake has long been my favorite American dessert, so it seemed natural to attempt one with Middle Eastern ingredients and flavors. Enter this raw, gluten-free, pistachio date beauty. With a chewy, caramelly base, a nutty and creamy filling and a sweet and crunchy topping, it's the dreamiest of desserts and can be frozen for up to two months. The combination of dates and cardamom in the bottom layer is reminiscent of desserts from the Arabian Peninsula, while the mixture of pistachio butter and cream cheese is evocative of Levantine flavors and the sweetened fruit on top is an homage to strawberry season back home.

YIELD: 8 SLICES

For the Base

1½ cups (120 g) gluten-free old-fashioned oats

½ cup (62 g) unsalted pistachios

½ cup (72 g) unsalted almonds

6 large Medjool dates, pitted

2 tbsp (28 g) vegan ghee or vegan butter

1 tsp ground cinnamon

¼ tsp ground cardamom

Pinch of sea salt

For the Filling

¾ cup (170 g) pistachio butter

1⅓ cups (298 g) vegan cream cheese

½ cup (115 g) plus 1 tbsp (20 g) vegan vanilla yogurt

¼ cup (55 g) solid coconut oil

4 Medjool dates, pitted

¼ cup (60 ml) maple syrup

1 tbsp (15 ml) lemon juice

For the Topping

1 cup (144 g) strawberries, halved or quartered

⅔ cup (99 g) blueberries

1 tbsp (15 ml) maple syrup

¼ cup (31 g) pistachios, chopped

Line the bottom and sides of an 8-inch (20-cm) springform pan with parchment paper.

To make the base, combine the oats, pistachios, almonds, dates, ghee, cinnamon, cardamom and salt in a food processor. Pulse it until the mixture sticks together when pinched. Press the base evenly onto the bottom of the springform pan and refrigerate it for 15 to 20 minutes.

To make the filling, combine the pistachio butter, cream cheese, yogurt, coconut oil, dates, maple syrup and lemon juice in a food processor. Pulse it until completely smooth and creamy. Pour the filling on top of the base and spread it evenly. Refrigerate the cheesecake for at least 6 hours or preferably overnight to set.

To make the topping, add the strawberries, blueberries and maple syrup to a medium-sized bowl. Toss to combine, then refrigerate the topping for 10 to 15 minutes, or until ready to eat. Arrange the fruit and chopped pistachios however you like when ready to serve. Store leftovers in the fridge for up to 4 days.

SALTED TAHINI CHOCOLATE CHIP COOKIES

Nowadays chocolate is pretty common in the Middle East and widely used in desserts. Similarly, the Middle East is home to a wide variety of cookies, from ghorayeba to ka'ak to ma'amoul. So I wanted to create a recipe centered on the cookie concept that featured chocolate in a Middle Eastern setting. I've always thought tahini and chocolate is such an underrated pairing, and these cookies prove just how good they can be together.

YIELD: ABOUT 20 LARGE COOKIES

½ cup (113 g) vegan butter, at room temperature

½ cup (125 g) runny tahini

⅔ cup (132 g) granulated sugar

⅓ cup (73 g) light brown sugar, packed

⅓ cup (80 ml) plant milk

1 tbsp (15 ml) vanilla extract

½ tbsp (6 g) ground cinnamon

1⅓ cups (165 g) all-purpose flour

1 tbsp (14 g) baking powder

1¾ cups (300 g) vegan dark chocolate chips, plus more to taste for topping

Flaky sea salt, to serve

Using an electric mixer, beat the butter, tahini, granulated sugar and brown sugar in a large bowl until creamy and fluffy, about 2 minutes. Add the milk, vanilla and cinnamon. Beat the mixture for 1 minute to combine.

In a separate bowl, sift together the flour and baking powder. Stir the dry ingredients into the wet ingredients using a spatula, until well incorporated. Fold in the chocolate chips. Refrigerate the cookie dough for at least 30 minutes.

Preheat the oven to 350°F (177°C) and line a sheet pan with parchment paper. Position a rack at the top of the oven.

Once ready, use an ice cream scoop to form a ball of cookie dough, place it on the sheet pan and slightly flatten it. Make sure to leave 2 inches (5 cm) between each cookie. Bake the cookies in batches on the top rack for 13 to 14 minutes, or until golden on the bottom but still soft on top.

The cookies will firm up as they cool. I like my cookies to be chewy, but if you'd like a harder cookie, bake them for 2 to 3 extra minutes. Transfer the cookies to a cooling rack as soon as you take them out of the oven. Let them cool for 5 minutes, then sprinkle the cookies with the salt and extra chocolate chips.

Enjoy immediately or let them cool completely. Store in an airtight container at room temperature for up to 3 days or in the fridge for up to 1 week.

ACKNOWLEDGMENTS

First and foremost, thanks to my wonderful husband, John, for having an endless amount of patience, doing more dishes than I can count, running to the store at a moment's notice to get me ingredients I kept forgetting and enduring my exhaustive questions following every recipe. For being the voice of reason when I was convinced I couldn't veganize one recipe or the other, for being willing to try just about any dish and for always believing in and praying for me. You're the best!

To my mom, Safaa, for cooking absolutely delicious food every single day despite working 60 hours a week and instilling the value of a home-cooked meal in me from a very young age. For teaching me—when I was a very snarly teenager—all the cooking basics and for meeting my very slow, very clumsy samboosa and mahshi rolling attempts with nothing but patience and praise. Thanks for being with me every step of my cooking journey, for taking the time to type recipes and answer questions on Messenger, for complimenting my tofu and seitan creations even though you have no idea what they are and for always giving honest feedback.

To my brother, Mahmoud, for not shying away from giving me constructive criticism on both my photography and recipe introductions and for always cheering me on.

To my sister-in-law, Leanna, for introducing me to vital wheat gluten by making the best vegan "chicken" nuggets I've ever had to this day—which ended up convincing me veganism wasn't restrictive—and for making and sharing countless plant-based dishes since. Many of the creations here were inspired by recipes you showed me.

To my in-laws, Debbie and Tommy, and my brother-in-law, Daniel, for their enthusiastic support and to all my little nieces and nephew, for being curious and giving my new concoctions a try, even when very doubtful you'll like them.

To Emily Archbold, Jenna Patton and my Page Street Publishing family for helping me bring this book to life and being fully on-board with the concept of veganizing Middle Eastern food.

To the wonderful foodie community on Instagram, including @janetsmunchmeals, @jackfruitfulkitchen, @betterfoodguru, @theroguebrusselsprout, @wanderingchickpea and @veganbowls, for all the encouragement and support they've provided over the years. I really wouldn't be here without you!

ABOUT THE AUTHOR

Noha Elbadry-Cloud is the recipe creator, writer and photographer behind @leeksnbeets on Instagram. Noha enjoys crafting recipes focused on showcasing the beauty of whole food plant-based eating, often with a Middle Eastern twist. In addition, she loves sharing quick, easy and delicious vegan meals in short videos. Her work has been featured in Vegan Bowls' cookbook *Simple Swaps* and on the Vegan Bowls website. It has also been featured on the Instagram accounts for the feedfeedvegan, THRIVE magazine, Best of Vegan and Pop Sugar. Aside from cooking and photography, Noha enjoys reading, hiking and working out. She currently lives in Magnolia, Arkansas, with her husband.

INDEX